Also of interest

Ethical Principles for Social Policy
Edited by John Howie

Ethical Principles and Practice
Edited by John Howie

ETHICAL ISSUES

IN

CONTEMPORARY SOCIETY

Edited by

John Howie and George Schedler

Southern Illinois University Press
Carbondale and Edwardsville

Library of Congress Cataloging-in-Publication Data

Ethical issues in contemporary society/edited by John Howie and
George Schedler.
   p.   cm.
Includes bibliographical references and index.
1. Social ethics.   I. Howie, John.   II. Schedler, George.
    HM216.E763   1995   94-15902
        303.3'72—dc20   CIP
            ISBN 0-8093-1971-3

Contents

Contributors

Tom Regan, professor of philosophy at North Carolina State University, is the author of *Understanding Philosophy* (1974), *All That Dwell Therein: Essays on Animal Rights and Environmental Ethics* (1982), *The Case for Animal Rights* (1983), *Bloomsbury's Prophet: The Moral Philosophy of G. E. Moore* (1987), and *The Thee Generation: Reflections on the Coming Revolution* (1991). He is the editor, coauthor, or coeditor of nine additional books, including *Matters of Life and Death* (1980), *Health Care Ethics: An Introduction* (1986), *And Justice for All: New Introductory Essays in Ethics and Social Policy* (with Donald VanDerVeer, 1986), and *Animal Sacrifices: Religious Perspectives on the Use of Animals in Science* (1988).

Carol C. Gould, professor in the Department of Humanities, Stevens Institute of Technology, is the author of *Rethinking Democracy: Freedom and Social Cooperation in Politics, Economy, and Society* (1988) and *Marx's Social Ontology: Individuality and Community in Marx's Theory of Social Reality* (1978). She is the editor of *Women and Philosophy: Toward A Theory of Liberation* (with Marx Wartofsky, 1976), *Beyond Domination: New Perspectives on Women and Philosophy* (1984), *The Information Web: Ethical and Social Implications of Computer Networking* (1989), and *Artifacts, Representations, and Social Practice* (with Robert S. Cohen, 1994). A member of Phi Beta Kappa, she is the recipient of a National Science Foundation Grant, a Fulbright Senior Scholar Award, a National Endowment for the Humanities Fellowship for College Teachers, and a Rockefeller Foundation Fellowship.

She has taught at the University of Pittsburgh, Swarthmore College, Herbert H. Lehman College (CUNY), and the State University of New York at New Paltz.

James Rachels, professor of philosophy at the University of Alabama at Birmingham, is the author of *The End of Life: Euthanasia and Morality* (1986), *The Elements of Philosophy* (2d ed., 1992), and *Created from Animals: The Moral Implications of Darwinism* (1990). He is the editor of *Moral Problems: A Collection of Philosophical Essays* (3d ed., 1978), *Understanding Moral Philosophy* (1976), *The Right Thing to Do* (1989), and *Philosophical Issues: A Contemporary Introduction* (with Frank Tillman, 1972). Recipient of a National Endowment for the Humanities Award (1973) and the Ireland Prize for Scholarly Distinction in the Arts and Sciences (1992), he has served as dean of humanities (1978–83) and acting vice president at the University of Alabama at Birmingham.

James P. Sterba, professor of philosophy at the University of Notre Dame, is the author of *The Demands of Justice* (1980), *How to Make People Just: A Practical Reconciliation of Alternative Conceptions of Justice* (1988), and *The Catholic Bishops and the Economy: A Debate* (with Douglas B. Rasmussen, 1987). He is the editor of *Justice: Alternative Political Perspectives* (1980), *Morality in Practice* (1994), *The Ethics of War and Nuclear Deterrence* (1984), *Contemporary Ethics: Selected Readings* (1989), *Social Philosophy Today* (1989), *Freedom, Equality, and Social Change: Philosophical Essays* (with Creighton Peden, 1989), *Ethics in the History of Western Philosophy* (with Robert J. Cavalier and James Gouinlock, 1989), and *Feminist Philosophies: Problems, Theories, and Applications* (with Janet A. Kourany and Rosemarie Tong, 1991).

Louis P. Pojman, professor of philosophy at the University of Mississippi, earned his D.Phil. from Oxford University and his Ph.D. from Union Theological Seminary. Awarded Kent, Fulbright, and Rockefeller fellowships, he is the author of *The Logic of Subjectivity: A Critique of Kierkegaard's Philosophy of Religion* (1984), *Religious Belief and the Will* (1986), *Ethics: Discovering Right and Wrong* (1990), and *Life and Death: Grappling with the Moral Dilemmas of Our Time* (1992). He is the editor of *Phi-*

losophy of Religion: An Anthology (1993), *Ethical Theory: Classical and Contemporary Readings* (1990), *Life and Death: A Reader* (1992), and *The Theory of Knowledge: Classical and Contemporary Readings* (1992).

David L. Norton, professor of philosophy at the University of Delaware, is the author of *Democracy and Moral Development* (1991), *Personal Destinies: A Philosophy of Ethical Individualism (1976),* and *Japanese Buddhism and the American Renaissance* (1993). He is the editor of *Philosophies of Love* (with Mary F. Kille, rev. ed., 1983). He is also the author of forty articles and a dozen reviews in scholarly journals and magazines. The recipient of an honorary doctorate degree from Soka University (Tokyo), he earned a masters degree in philosophy from Washington University (1962) and a Ph.D. from Boston University (1968). In addition to his articles on education and moral philosophy, he has written and spoken extensively on Thoreau's philosophy.

Acknowledgments

It is a pleasure to acknowledge openly the assistance, encouragement, and support provided for the editing and publication of this volume of Leys Lectures.

The Wayne Leys Memorial Lectureship Fund, under the management of the Southern Illinois University Foundation, with assistance from a philosophy departmental committee, sponsors each year a special lecture by an outstanding philosopher. This is the third group of six such lectures showing the relevance of ethics to contemporary issues. As embodiments of this concern, they comprise an appropriate living memorial to Wayne A. R. Leys.

Tom Regan's essay "Feminism and Vivisection" was published by Temple University Press as chapter 5, pp. 83–103, in Regan's book *The Thee Generation: Reflections on the Coming Revolution* © 1991 by Temple University. It is reprinted as chapter 1 by permission of Temple University Press. Originally it was presented as the third of four annual Gilbert Ryle Lectures at Trent University, Peterborough, Ontario (1988).

Portions of Carol C. Gould's essay "Positive Freedom, Economic Justice, and the Redefinition of Democracy" are reprinted in chapter 2 with the permission of Gould and Cambridge University Press. Some of the content of this essay appears in Gould's book *Rethinking Democracy: Freedom and Social Cooperation in Politics, Economy, and Society* © 1988 by Cambridge University Press.

Portions of chapter 5 appeared earlier in Louis P. Pojman's

article "Do Animal Rights Entail Moral Nihilism?" *Public Affairs Quarterly* (April 1993) and are reprinted in chapter 5 with the permission of Pojman and *Public Affairs Quarterly*.

The three remaining chapters, by James Rachels, James P. Sterba, and David L. Norton, are all published here for the first time.

Special thanks are expressed to Sharon Langrand for her care and efficiency in typing and correcting the manuscript and to Professor Angela Rubin of Morris Library for gracious assistance and cheerfulness in the tiresome task of completing notes and bibliographical entries. The early and assured support of Dean John S. Jackson, College of Liberal Arts, was greatly appreciated.

Introduction

Gender bias, racial prejudice, economic injustice, the exploitative use of animals, a naive moral relativism, and the failure of public education are all ethical issues that contemporary society confronts. Considered in their broader context, these issues are the focus of the chapters in this book.

With the traditional Western conception of the person as its foundation, liberal feminism, as Tom Regan indicates in chapter 1, challenges the social and legal impediments prohibiting women from receiving equality of treatment. These feminists ask, Why should a radically disproportionate number of men be offered an opportunity to receive an education, become property owners, pursue their interests outside the home, and make major contributions to commerce, art, technology, law, and literature? For these feminists the major task is to eliminate this disparity and correct these inequities.

A more radical feminism, an ethic-of-care approach, rejects outright this Western conception as itself masculinized or patriarchal. It insists that the whole ideology of male distinctiveness and superiority to other animals must be destroyed. This approach ascribes more importance to nurturing and sustaining interpersonal relationships rather than to rights and duties. The relationships of parent to child, friend to friend, and lover to lover are those worth developing. If they cannot be avoided, conflicts are resolved in mutually beneficial or enhancing ways.

By means of a "consistency argument," Regan extends

this ethic-of-care feminism to persons and animals outside our inner group of interpersonal relationships. To the extent that these other persons and animals are relevantly similar to us, consistency requires we include them in our circle of care. And, after all, pain, suffering, and untimely death are impartially undesirable, whatever being undergoes them. But, Regan notes, adopting this consistency argument dulls the radical edge of this approach, since it now includes the patriarchal element of reason.

In Regan's view animals used in scientific research, regardless of its exact nature, are treated as simply means for human purposes. No law protects them from pain, suffering, or untimely death once they are in the scientific context. Animals are treated in ways that directly conflict with Regan's supplemented ethic of care. Consistency requires that humans and nonhumans be considered morally equal. And this means minimally that we not permit to be done to animals "in the name of science" what we would not allow to be done to our fellow human beings. This feminism must "abhor vivisection" just as nature abhors a vacuum.

What rethinking of democracy in terms of freedom and equality is required by economic justice? Carol C. Gould offers an answer to this question in chapter 2. Economic justice, she argues, requires that workers control the production process as well as the distribution process.

To make this justice possible, equal positive freedom is essential. This means sustaining an equal right to the conditions required for self-development, including enabling social and material conditions, as well as supporting political rights and civil liberties. Freedom, traditionally conceived as the absence of constraint, ignores these enabling conditions and omits the conception of freedom as self-development over time. Positive freedom, Gould notes, has three elements: (1) capacity for choice and its exercise, (2) absence of constraining conditions, and (3) the availability of "means." By "means" is meant the requisite material and social conditions. Material conditions include means of subsistence, enabling conditions of labor, and

appropriate leisure activity. Social conditions include cooperative forms of social interaction, reciprocal recognition of free
agency, and suitable access to education and various social institutions.

A plausible redefinition of democracy requires extending
it to cover decision making in economic and social contexts
essential to self-development. For such development a wide
range of options should be possible. It is becoming the person
one chooses by actualizing one's purposes and meeting one's
needs. Many different social conditions are indispensable for
such comprehensive self-development.

Economic justice, in addition to self-management, requires property rights and ownership by workers. A socialist
market structure in which labor is not a commodity will replace
a capitalist one and will, Gould insists, make economic justice
an attainable goal.

Taking racial prejudice as his paradigm, James Rachels
explores in chapter 3 the deeper meaning of prejudice and what
equality of treatment involves. It is a commonplace in ethics
that people should receive equal treatment. But troublesome
questions arise as to what constitutes equal treatment and
which administrators are minimally free of prejudice to dis-
pense it. Obviously, it is not a resolution of the problem to insist
that all people are equal—taken descriptively, this proposal is
simply false. Nor will it do to say that people, despite their
natural and acquired differences, are to be treated as though
they were equal. Equality may perhaps be a normative presumption in the absence of relevant differences.

What justifies unequal treatment? Any difference in treatment must be based on a relevant difference in the situation.
Without offering a complete theory of relevant differences,
Rachels provides valuable guidelines for answering this question.

Prejudicial reasoning, Rachels indicates, is subtle (even
unconscious) and insidious. People often do benefit from treating other people prejudicially. And it is far too easy for myths
to develop and offer fictitious differences for actual discrimina-

tory practices. Stereotypes, unconscious bias, and the human knack for rationalizing make it difficult even for people of good will to prevent prejudice from influencing their actions.

In chapter 4 James P. Sterba invites us to consider the different and more general problem of how to persuade people to act for moral reasons. A first step is taken once a person understands the implausibility of moral relativism. It is implausible because some alleged divergences in moral views are only apparent and not actual, because it is not always the same act that is morally approved in one society and morally condemned in another, and because relativism cannot tell us, with supporting reasons, which group or individual is to serve as the standard of reference for its relativity. Moreover, relativism makes an absolutistic claim for the truth of its own point of view. And, a person may ask, if the truth thus asserted is not relativistic, why should the good be relativistic?

Having indicated that moral relativism is rationally bankrupt, Sterba proposes an alternative account by which he hopes to persuade people to be moral "by force of argument." This he expects to do by showing that morality is a requirement of rationality and that it is impartial in its practical requirements.

The essential conflict between self-interested and altruistic reasons rationally conceived can be resolved on a piecemeal basis. Sometimes priority should be given to self-interested reasons, and sometimes priority should be given to altruistic reasons. This helps people to avoid a question-begging justification for either of the two conflicting alternatives.

The right to welfare and the right to equal opportunity (or, as Sterba calls them, "the welfare liberal ideal") offers a fusion of practical ends for five ideals—liberty (as espoused by libertarians), fairness (as professed by welfare liberals), common good (as proclaimed by communitarians), androgyny (as proclaimed by feminists), and equality (as defended by socialists).

Do animals have "rights?" Do persons have moral obligations to animals? Louis P. Pojman, in chapter 5, seeks to answer both these questions through a critical examination of seven theories of the moral status of animals. Three of these give animals little or no status; one grants animals substantial, but not equal, status; and the remaining three grant animals some kind of equal status with us. These last three are all called egalitarian, and it is these that Pojman wishes to show entail a moral nihilism. This is the view that there are no moral duties at all.

As Pojman explains, Peter Singer, a moderate egalitarian, holds that an act is moral if it satisfies the largest combination of preferences. In assessing preferences, animals and humans count equally. Singer's view is that of a nonspeciesist "preference utilitarianism." In this view the pleasure and pain experienced by sentient beings must be taken into account. Rational, self-conscious beings are, however, more valuable than beings without these abilities. To kill them is a greater wrong than to exterminate a merely sentient being. Hence, Singer's egalitarianism, on further analysis, is simply a principle of impartiality. Moreover, it is difficult to determine how, on Singer's view, one would assess the preferences of chickens, cows, and pigs against those of self-conscious persons.

For Pojman the radical egalitarianism of Regan and Taylor, by expanding without limit its egalitarianism, makes everything equally valuable and undercuts differences essential to value itself. Thus, like other forms of egalitarianism, it leads to nihilism. To replace this "dead" egalitarianism, Pojman offers a moral philosophy based on reciprocity and merit. Animals possess no natural "rights" since they are unable to enter into contracts. However, animals do deserve to be treated kindly, and we need to eliminate cruelty in animal factories and should even abandon some animal research for scientific purposes.

For David L. Norton in chapter 6, one of our most pressing problems is the failure of our educational system. It is an ethical issue of great concern because our educational system is failing to enable our students to make wise "life-shaping" choices. And it is these life-shaping choices that create moral character. Such important choices include vocational choice, choice of whether to marry and whom to marry, choice of whether to have children and how many to have, and choice of friends, to name only a few.

Symptomatic of this deeper problem are the poor test performances over the last several years by U.S. students in reading, writing, mathematics, and science. But to focus on test taking for whatever immediate improvement might result is to overlook the deeper problem for two reasons: (1) skill at test taking cannot readily be converted into resourcefulness in tackling tough human problems, and (2) the educational problem is deep-rooted and requires nothing less than recapturing and rekindling the eagerness of students to learn. The present system tends to extinguish spontaneity and the joy of learning by its bureaucracy, depersonalization, and authoritarian approaches. Grades, credits, honors, and diplomas (all external rewards) take the place of intrinsic satisfactions, such as curiosity satisfied and wonder enhanced. Scientific management and efficiency have been emphasized to the exclusion of student initiatives and creativity.

For Norton, making wise, life-shaping choices involves several important necessary conditions, including self-knowledge. This self-knowledge includes direct acquaintance with vocational alternatives and the firsthand experience of actually doing something for others. Both these experiences provide the "personal truths" essential to worthy living. Worthy living realizes objective value while at the same time being self-fulfilling for the individual within society.

Chapters in this book consider in their own way live moral issues confronting contemporary society. Reflective readers will discover through them clues to a better understanding of these issues, and hints for solving the accompanying problems.

John Howie

ETHICAL ISSUES
IN
CONTEMPORARY SOCIETY

1

Feminism and Vivisection

Tom Regan

Feminism takes more than one form and has more than one voice. I shall not be able to consider all of them. If I am sensible, this fact will chasten the confidence with which I reach my conclusions. Whatever form feminism takes, and with whatever voice the philosophy is spoken, we do best, I think, to ask how it responds to a recurring conception of the human person in Western moral and political thought—a conception that, while it hardly is lacking in critics, nevertheless is so pervasive that I think it appropriate to refer to it as the "traditional" conception. This is the conception we find in such diverse thinkers as Thomas Hobbes, John Stuart Mill, John Locke, and Immanuel Kant, for example. Permit me to begin by sketching the main features of this widely shared view.

The Traditional Conception

The first point to note is the great emphasis these theorists place on rationality, not only its presence in normal humans, but also its value or importance. Hobbes's normative theory is a case in point. How are we to make our escape from the state of nature? Not by means of our brute force. Not by the pouring forth of feelings of sympathy, empathy, compassion, friendship, and love. No, given our selfish nature, it is only by means of our reason that we can set ourselves free of the "brutish" existence to which otherwise we are heirs. Mill, too, despite the many differences between his theory and Hobbes's, is enthusiastically on Hobbes's side when it comes to the place of reason in human life. It is reason, after all, that separates us from pigs, with whom we share an emotional kinship, and it is owing largely to our ability to take pleasure in the exercise of our rational capacities that we are able to forge a life that is really worth living—a life that cultivates the mind, not one that indulges the body. As for a natural rights theorist such as John Locke, we are not surprised to learn that in his view only rational beings can have natural rights. Nor are we shocked when we discover that in Kant's theory the only individuals to whom we can have direct moral duties are individuals like us: rational beings. Indeed, in Kant's theory, our right acts have no moral worth at all if we perform them only because we want to do so; what worth they have is due exclusively to our exercising rational control, especially in the face of contrary desires. In all these theories, then, our identity as rational creatures is both affirmed and greatly valued, while at the same time our identity as physical beings, with roots in the biology of the past and entanglements with the ecology of the present, tends to be either entirely ignored or greatly minimized.

This celebration of reason over emotional and other noncognitive capacities can be purchased only at the price of denigrating the importance or value of these latter capacities. Feelings are not to be trusted; reason is. The emotions are to be—indeed, must be—controlled, and it is reason alone that is equal to the task. The carnal lusts of the body must be put in their place—must be tamed—and it is reason that cracks the whip. Present in all the theories, this denigration of our nonrational nature is perhaps most evident in Kant's, according to which reason is understood as a capacity of what he calls our "noumenal self," a power that transcends the natural world and

operates freely of causal determinism. In these and other variations on this main theme, we see that it is our connectedness
with the rest of nature that is identified with that part of us that
needs to be controlled or tamed. It is nature, expressing itself
through our body, that requires a ruler; and it is what separates
us from the rest of nature—our mind, our reason—that is assigned the task of trainer and controller. The wages of the body
are sin. In reason alone lies salvation.

Along with this celebration of reason (the mind) over feelings or emotions (the body), we find a collateral celebration of
the objective over the subjective. The standard of right conduct
for me cannot be any different than the standard of right conduct for you, anymore than the sum of 2 + 3 can differ between
us. While Kant locates this objective standard in the test of
universalizability (what he calls "the categorical imperative"),
Mill offers the principle of utility; and whereas Hobbes fixes
the standard of right conduct in those rules agreed upon by
persons in the state of nature, Locke grounds morality in the
universal "rights of Man." In every case, however, it is assumed
that there is one—and only one—objective, impartial, abstract,
universal basis of morality, the same for all people, at all times,
and in all places. And since it is only reason, not our feelings
or emotions, that can be counted upon to discover such a basis
and, once having discovered it, apply it, it is dispassionate,
objective reason, not passionate, subjective feelings, that must
guide us morally.

This theme of the desirability of domination by reason
goes beyond the inner biographical struggles of individuals
with themselves. It also gets played out when human nature is
contrasted with nature generally. Nature is wild, treacherous,
"nasty" (to use Hobbes's memorable description). Not only our
own desires but nature itself needs to be controlled, tamed,
domesticated, and made to cooperate. Hobbes's acceptance of
these views is perhaps the most obvious, but Locke, too, is a
partisan. It is only after we humans have "mixed our labor"
with some part of nature, only after we have taken it into ourselves as our "property," that it attains what value it has. For
both Mill and Kant, moreover, though the natural world can

be and sometimes is a source of aesthetic pleasure, awe, wonder, and sublimity, it nevertheless lacks all these values apart
from the appreciation of a human observer. Despite their many
differences, therefore, all four of the major thinkers we have
considered agree that nature has no value apart from human
presence or use. It is we humans who give value to nature,
especially through our use of our reason. It is mainly by the
imposition of rational control over the natural world, done in
the name of advancing our own and other human interests, and
expressive of our achievements as cultural beings, that makes
nature valuable.

Notice, further, how the spirit, if not the letter, of Hobbes's
view, when interpreted as a historical thesis, remains alive in
the other thinkers. It is, of course, false that humans lived the
solitary existence Hobbes depicts. Everyone knows this. And
yet each of the theories under review harkens back to that myth.
We find this in Locke's emphasis on "the rights of Man"—of
individual members of the species Homo sapiens, that is. And
we also find it in Mill's celebrated "proof" of the principle of
utility: it is, he argues, because a person desires his or her own
pleasure and views it as good, that a person must desire that
everyone have pleasure, and view that as very good indeed.
And as for Kant, the noumenal self, which is the source of all
freedom and worth in human life, transcends the physical
world and, as such, can carry out its deliberations and make
its decisions as if it existed quite alone, in a timeless vacuum.
In sum, when all the dust settles, it is the interests, the pleasures, the freedom, or the rights of discrete, individual human
beings, abstracted from their biological relationships to the natural world and their cultural relationships to the society in
which they actually live, on which the fundamental principles
of morality ultimately depend, according to the theories discussed above. And thus it is that, despite the demonstrable
falsity of Hobbes's description of the state of nature, interpreted
historically, these several moral philosophies continue to per-
petuate the vision of individual human beings as "solitary"
creatures—atoms of reason abstracted from their incidental biological and cultural molecular structure.

Just one final similarity should be noted. This concerns the normative role played by the idea of impartiality. To judge impartially is not to allow any personal factor to prejudice one's judgment. Judges would do this, for example, if they decided guilt or innocence on the basis of how well they knew those charged with breaking the law, how much they liked them, or what the judges stood to gain as a result of the verdicts they rendered. All four of the thinkers considered to this point are of one mind in disallowing partiality in the making of moral judgments—Locke in his affirmation of the basic rights of all humans; Mill in his brave demand that everyone's pleasures and pains must be considered and counted equitably; Hobbes in his insistence that the rules of morality be fairly applied to everyone; and Kant in his categorical requirement that every one of us must ask whether our individual maxims can be universalized, that is, whether everyone could act as we do, for the same reasons we have. In a word, morality for all four thinkers requires the defeat of partiality and the triumph of impartiality.

Here, then, we have, by way of summary, the recurring image of the human person—the individual human being—that has characterized so much of Western moral and political thought. Each of us is by nature selfish, innately predisposed to look out for only our own good. Moreover, this deeply rooted selfishness is expressed by our standing apart from, rather than in our being a part of, a biological, ecological, or social community. Indeed, the most fundamental task we all face is how to meld our natural appetite for our individual good into the larger fabric of life, especially human society. The solution to this problem is not to be found in our emotions or feelings, which are irrational and liable to mislead us and which in any event we share with many other animals. Instead, it is to be found in our ability to reason, which is unique to the human species. Once this is understood, the key to unlocking the essence of a good human life also is apparent. This is to be found in cultivating that which is uniquely human—our reason, or more generally, our mind. Only in this way can we overcome the limitations placed on our fulfillment by the body and its demands. This triumph of the mind over the body also carries over into our dealings with the natural world, which may be viewed as a kind of shared body, standing no less in need of being tamed and domesticated than our individual physicality. The successful domestication of nature, in which we may all take part, is what is known as culture. The greater the triumph over nature, the higher the culture; the less so, the more "primitive" the culture and the people comprising it. In the particular case of a fully developed moral life, growth lies in the direction of objectivity as opposed to subjectivity, impartiality as opposed to partiality, and—of course—reason as opposed to emotion.

Liberal Feminism

Some feminist thinkers are not critical of the views I have just summarized. For these thinkers the problem lies not in these views (not in the traditional conception) but in how women have been denied those very things that are essential to a good, full human life, given this conception of the human person. Mary Wollstonecraft speaks admirably for this wing of feminist thinkers, arguing in her classic 1792 work *A Vindication of the Rights of Woman* that women are no more lacking in the uniquely human characteristics than are men.

> In what does man's [that is, humanity's] pre-eminence over the brute creation, consist? The answer is as clear as that a half is less than a whole, in Reason. . . . For what purpose were the passions implanted? That man by struggling with them might attain a degree of knowledge denied of the brutes.
>
> Consequently the perfection of our nature and capability of happiness must be estimated by the degree of reason, virtue and humanity that distinguish the individual and that from the exercise of reason, knowledge and virtue naturally flow.[1]

The mention of "virtues" should not be misunderstood. Commenting on Wollstonecraft's thought, the Australian philosopher Val Plumwood remarks that "*masculine* virtues are taken to be *human* virtues, what distinguishes humans from the sphere of nature, especially the qualities of rationality, transcendence and freedom. . . . The human character ideal she [Wollstonecraft] espouses diverges sharply from the feminine character ideal, which she rejects, 'despising that weak elegancy of mind, exquisite sensibility, and sweet docility of manners.' Instead, she urges that women become 'more masculine and respectable.' "[2]

That "masculinity" would find expression in power and domination, a point not lost on Amelia Bloomer, who, writing in the nineteenth century, asserts that "he [man] has brought the Bible to prove that he is her [woman's] lord and master, and taught her that resistance to his authority is to resist God's will." "I deny that the Bible teaches any such doctrine," Bloomer asserts, concluding, "God made them different in sex, but equal in intellect, and gave them equal dominion."[3] When it comes to domination, it seems, two can play as well as one.

As these representative quotations from Wollstonecraft and Bloomer show, some feminist thinkers are prepared to work with the traditional concept of the human person rather than to challenge it. What they do challenge are those social and legal impediments that stand in the way of equality of treatment of both women and men, a concept of justice at the very heart of the liberal tradition in Western political thought, which helps to explain the appropriateness of the name now commonly applied to this strain of feminist thought—"liberal feminism."

To a limited degree, liberal feminists have succeeded in achieving some of their goals. Educational and career opportunities, for example, formerly closed to women, increasingly are open to them. Some thinkers (sometimes called "sexual conservatives") are of the opinion that liberal feminists already have gone too far. But other thinkers within the feminist movement in philosophy believe that liberal feminists have not gone far enough. Indeed, the very things liberal feminists would point to as part of the solution—things like greater educational and professional opportunities for women, for example—in the eyes of some feminists actually are seen as part of feminism's major problem.

The Feminist Critique of Liberal Feminism

Those feminists who are critical of the liberal position are a mixed group, with no univocal voice or identity. I will not be able to discuss all of them. But allow me briefly to sketch a common line of criticism they raise against liberal feminism.

According to these critics, it is not enough that women be able to compete equitably with men for educational opportunities, jobs, pay, or social and professional benefits. All that these changes would achieve, were they to occur, is what Ariel Salleh has described as the "masculinizing" of feminism.[4] Val Plumwood explains this idea when she writes that

> the problem for women [according to liberal feminism] was to claim full *humanity* i.e., conform to the main human character ideal, defined by traits characteristic also of the masculine, and to fit into, adapt themselves to, the corresponding social institutions of the public sphere. These might require some minor modification but basically it was women who were to change and adapt, (sometimes with help) and women (or what society had made of them) who were the problem. The position can be summed up as that of demanding equal participation in a masculine concept or ideal of humanity, and the associated activist strategy as that of demanding equal admittance for women to a masculine-defined sphere and masculine institutions.[5]

Anyone reading this will have noticed how heavy-laden with the word *masculine* this passage from Plumwood is—"masculine institutions," "masculine-defined sphere," "masculine concept or ideal of humanity." Why does she express herself in these terms? One way of answering this question, I think, is as follows.

Historically, in Western civilization at least, it has been men—not all men, of course, but, in comparison with women, a greatly disproportionate number of them—who have been

afforded opportunities to receive an education, thereby cultivating their minds; it has been men who have been given the
freedom to "mix their labor" with nature and thereby come to
be property owners; it has been men who have been encour-
aged to pursue their interests outside the home, wherever they
may lead; and it has been men who have been in a position to
make major contributions to our culture. Women, by contrast,
have been assigned the roles of satisfying men's sexual needs
(as "sex objects") and of running the home (without pay) and
raising the children (again without pay), with the result that,
comparatively speaking, few have been able to acquire property, pursue their interests beyond the home, secure an education or job that was comparable to a man's, or contribute in
large numbers to the forging of our culture—to our art, commerce, religion, technology, law, literature, and (alas) philosophy.

Viewed against the backdrop of the ideas presented earlier, what we can see, then, is that men, to a vastly greater
extent than women, have been given opportunities to realize
the sort of good, full human life that emanates from acceptance
of the traditional conception of the human person. The interpretation of this fact offered by such thinkers as Ariel Salleh is
that this traditional conception of the human individual and
the allied one of a good, full human life are not the sexually
unbiased, objective, impartial views they might at first appear
to be; on the contrary, they are sexually biased, discriminatory,
ideological views of what men think the human person is or
can be, and of what a good, full human life is, if you are male.
Only instead of these normative beliefs being put forward in
this plain, frank language, they are expressed in the language
of humanity, embodying an ideal of a good, full human life for
all human beings. The message is clear: men are the measure
of all things—or, at least, of these things.

The upshot is that the kind of life that historically has
been available to most women has been viewed as vastly less
than a good, full human life. And the virtues traditionally associated with womankind—the virtues associated with nurturing children and sustaining a home, those identified with em-

pathy, sympathy, compassion, gentleness, and the "softer" emotional side of human nature—normally have been relegated to a very low standing by men, as virtues no man would (or should) value in another man or desire in himself. Small wonder, then, that thinkers like Wollstonecraft, herself enraptured by the traditional conception of the human person, would abjure the "feminine" virtues and encourage her "sisters" to become "more masculine and respectable." Once the traditional conception is accepted, the only way women have to achieve a truly worthwhile life is to emulate the ways and virtues traditionally open to men—for example, cultivating their reason (as opposed to their "exquisite sensibility") and claiming their fair share of the right to dominate nature by owning parts of it.

Thus we are able to understand why Plumwood expresses herself in the way she does (her use of such expressions as "masculine institutions" and "masculine concept or ideal of humanity," for example) and why feminists like Salleh wish to part company with the liberal feminist position. In the simplest possible terms, Salleh and the other feminists she represents believe that liberal feminism is not a true feminism but is, rather, a "masculinism"—a case of women trying to adjust themselves to male categories, male values, male institutions, and the expectations of (to use a word much favored in feminist literature) patriarchy. At the risk of oversimplification, but in the interests of simplicity, I shall refer to this wing of feminism as *ethic-of-care feminism*.

Ethic-of-Care Feminism

One way to approach this wing of feminism is to begin with some observations by Marilyn French. French sees in the liberal feminist's acceptance of the traditional conception of the human person the regrettable acceptance of patriarchy. In her view a true feminism must reject patriarchy, not adjust itself to it. She writes:

> Patriarchy is an ideology founded on the assumption that man is distinct from the animal and superior to it. The basis

of this superiority is man's contact with a higher power/ knowledge called god, reason, or control. The reason for man's existence is to shed all animal residue and realize fully his "divine" nature, the part that *seems* unlike any part owned by animals—mind, spirit, or control. In the process of achieving this, man has attempted to subdue nature both outside and inside himself; he has created a substitute environment in which he appears to be no longer dependent upon nature. The aim of the most influential minds has been to create an entirely factitious world, a world dominated by man, the one creature in control of his own destiny. This world, if complete, would be entirely in man's control . . . , and man himself would have eradicated or concealed his basic bodily and emotional bonds to nature.[6]

When French says that patriarchy as an ideology is "founded" on the assumptions of "man's" distinctness from and superiority to "the animals," she means, I think, that the other features of a patriarchal view of the world—for example, the celebration of reason over emotion, and of the mind over the body—are natural (though not necessarily logical) outgrowths of this more basic assumption. Thus, to attack patriarchy at its root would be to attack it at this point—the point where it is assumed that "*man*" is "distinct from the animal and superior to it." And this in turn is to say that the object of critical scrutiny is and must be the traditional conception of the human person.

Two very different lines of criticism can be pursued here. The first insists that women, no less than men, are "distinct from the animal and superior to it." This is the line of criticism we find in Mary Wollstonecraft and in other feminists who argue for the equality of women with men and who call for fairer, more equitable treatment for women. In other words, this is the familiar trail blazed by liberal feminists, a trail that in Ariel Salleh's telling phrase can only lead to the "masculinizing" of feminism, if feminism stops there. For Ariel Salleh and other feminists, however, a true feminism cannot stop there. A true feminism must dismantle the ideology of patriarchy, not only at its branches, so to speak—not only, that is, in those laws and social practices that discriminate unfairly against women—but root and all. And this means—or so I believe—that a true feminism must disassociate itself from the basic assumptions of patriarchy, including the one identified by Marilyn French: that "man is distinct from the animal and superior to it."

The Ethic of Care

The beginning of this disassociation lies in our acceptance of our animality. Social by nature we may be (as Aristotle observes and, on one interpretation, Hobbes contests), but animal we most certainly are. This is not to demean ourselves, not to make ourselves something less than what we are. Or, rather, the very thought that, in acknowledging and accepting our animality, we are demeaning or lessening ourselves—this very thought is itself a symptom of the ideology that needs uprooting.

But now there is a problem. Indeed, now there are quite a few problems. I shall explore only two. To begin with, if the abandonment of patriarchy really does involve not only acceptance of our animality but also rejection of our superiority over all other animals who lack a soul, or reason, or control, then we presumably must come to acknowledge our moral equality with those animals who are otherwise like us—that is, those animals who are conscious of the world, not only present in it; who, like us, respond to the world emotionally (through fear and anxiety, for example); and who can be pleased or pained by what happens to them. Thus, if an enlightened feminist perspective would find it wrong to make a human animal suffer or to cause a human fear or anxiety in a given context, it seems that this same perspective must make the same finding if a nonhuman animal is made to suffer or is caused fear or anxiety in a similar context. As I say, this *seems* to be the case. The first problem I want to address is how, viewed from a feminist perspective, this can be the case.

The moral status of nonhuman animals poses at least two problems for many feminist philosophers. First, there is the notable influence exercised by Carol Gilligan and her feminist moral theory—her "ethic of care," which she distinguishes from the patriarchal moral traditions of individual rights and duties.[7] There is much about Gilligan's views and the debates they have engendered that I am unable to recount and assess on this occasion. Suffice it to say here that if we accept the ethic of care as our ruling paradigm, we will naturally emphasize the importance of nurturing and sustaining existing interpersonal relationships (for example, those between parent and child, friend and friend, lover and lover). We will try to avoid conflicts, and when they do arise, we will try to find mutually beneficial ways to resolve them.

This is all well and good, as far as it goes. But does it go far enough? In particular, what are the resources within the ethic of care that can move people to consider the ethics of their dealings with individuals who stand outside the existing circle of their valued interpersonal relationships? Clearly, the resources seem to depend entirely on how much one cares for these individuals. And yet this seems to be such a contingent, such a chancy, basis for such an important moral idea. The very bonds of caring that unite us with some divide us from others. It is certainly possible that we should care about what happens to some individuals when in fact we do not care at all. And unless we supplement the ethic of care with some other motivating force—some other grounding of our moral judgment—we run the grave risk that our ethic will be excessively conservative and will blind us to those obligations we have to people toward whom we are indifferent.

Nowhere, perhaps, is this possibility more evident than in the case of our moral dealings with nonhuman animals. The plain fact is, most people do not care very much about what happens to nonhuman animals, or, if they do care, their care seems to be highly selective, limited to "pet" animals or to cuddly or rare specimens of wildlife, for example. What, then, becomes of the animals toward whom people are indifferent, given the ethic of care? Notice that we cannot say—what I find it natural to say—that we *ought* to care for these animals, that we have a *duty* to care for them, and, indeed, that they have a *right* to our protection. To speak in these natural ways—in the language of individual rights and duties—is out of bounds given the ethic of care, and it is out of bounds because it is supposed to be a veiled expression of patriarchy.

But if these ways of speaking are ruled out and if the moral ties that bind us to others are those defined by the ethic of care, then it seems doubtful that we will have the resources within our theory to be able to move people from their current attitudes of indifference regarding nonhuman animals to new, more caring ones. And thus it is that a feminist ethic that is limited to an ethic of care will, I think, be unable to illuminate the moral significance of the idea that we (human) animals are not superior to all other animals—and that, indeed, we and they are moral equals. For where the care is unequal and the vocabulary of duties and rights has no voice, one's ethical options seem to be exhausted. This cannot be a salutary situation for the ethic of care.

A Place for Reason in Ethics

That is the first problem the moral status of nonhuman animals poses for ethic-of-care feminism. The second problem arises when we stop to consider ways in which the circle of care might be extended to include these animals. One way—though perhaps not the only, or even the best, way—in which this might be done is by having recourse to what I call *consistency arguments*. The point of such arguments is to highlight the moral arbitrariness of excluding some individuals from the circle of one's moral concern. For example, pain is pain, wheresoever it may be, and the untimely death of anyone, especially the innocent, prima facie makes the world less good than it otherwise would have been. Granted, we care about pain and death most when those who suffer or die are close to us, and perhaps some people care even more when it is their own suffering and death they must confront. And yet this caring about the pain and death of another would not make sense if pain and untimely death themselves were unimportant. These great evils are prima facie undesirable apart from the particular identities of those who suffer and those who die.

This much granted, reason is now empowered to demonstrate the arbitrariness of the limits imposed by an ethic of care. Suppose it is true that we do not care much about the pain and death of strangers—for example, the pain and death of the many homeless people eking out a life (an *existence* would be closer to the truth) on the streets of major urban areas. Our presumed indifference toward them is not a sufficient reason to deny that we have any obligations to them. Since pain and an untimely death are undesirable apart from the particular identities of those who suffer or die, they are no less undesirable if those who suffer and die are strangers than if they are friends. Our obligation to help others, therefore—for example, to prevent their avoidable suffering—holds whether we care about or are indifferent to the one who needs our assistance. Perhaps it is true that we are more likely to succeed in helping those people we know best (our friends or our children, for example), and perhaps it is also true that, in many cases, our most stringent obligations are to those with whom we have a valued interpersonal relationship. But this cannot be the whole of morality. The moral universe is not circumscribed by the caring universe. In many cases reason shows that we should help another, even when we do not care for that individual.

This same kind of argument (a consistency argument) also can be marshaled in the case of the moral status of nonhuman animals. For if pain and an untimely death are undesirable in the case of humans, whatever their identities, then the same must be true of relevantly similar nonhuman animals, whatever their identities. In this way, then, an ethic of care can seek to overcome its conservative tendencies and to illuminate how nonhuman animals can gain entry to the moral community, as beings who are to be protected by some of the same principles that are to protect human beings, even if we do not care about what happens to them.

Moreover, advocates of an ethic of care can attempt to achieve these normative results without renouncing the importance of care in a fully developed moral life. Indeed, one might even urge (as I am inclined to do) that one of the great challenges the ethic of care places before us is to bring our caring into line with our reason, in the sense that in time we do care about the pain and death of those for whom reason informs us that we should care.

This way of addressing the first problem sketched above—the problem feminists face if they attempt to challenge the doctrine of human superiority while relying on the ethic of care—creates a second problem for these thinkers. For if the most (or at least a) satisfactory way to overcome the moral conservatism of the ethic of care, especially as this regards the assault on human chauvinism, is to make use of consistency arguments, then the feminist critique of patriarchy may not be as radical as some might wish it to be. For since these arguments by their very nature involve appeals to reason and abstract principles of logic, and since such principles and appeals are by their very nature partially definitive of the traditional conception of the human person (the very conception judged to be patriarchal to the core), it emerges that ethic-of-care feminists themselves must traffic with identifiable elements of the very prejudice they seek to overthrow.

To put the point more simply, these feminists face an unavoidable dilemma: either their ethical theory lacks the theoretical wherewithal to mount the desired attack on human chauvinism, or it contains the means to mount this attack. If the former, then the theory is deficient because of the barrenness of claims to human superiority. If the latter, then the theory is still deficient, judged by its own standards, since in this case it must incorporate elements of the very conception (the patriarchal conception) of the human person that it seeks to replace. Of the two alternatives, the latter is the least damaging and, therefore, is the one that I believe ethic-of-care feminists should accept. But whichever option is chosen, ethic-of-care feminism cannot be as radical as some might wish it to be.

Ethic-of-Care Feminism and Animal Liberation

Suppose I am right that ethic-of-care feminists are at liberty to use consistency arguments to wage their attack on the sort of human chauvinism that is indigenous to a patriarchal understanding of the world. If this much is granted, then we are in a position to ask what views these feminists should have concerning human interactions with nonhuman animals, if not in general, then in some more or less clearly defined context— say, the use humans make of nonhuman animals in science. To answer this question, we first need to offer a general characterization of how these animals are used in science.

This characterization is simple and straightforward. Whether the scientific interest be that of basic or applied research, whether it be product testing or the imparting of knowledge, these animals are treated as mere means to certain ends— ends chosen by individual scientists, usually with society's blessing. The animals are spoken of as "tools," "models," and the like, a vocabulary that even to this day continues to reflect the Cartesian view that nonhuman animals are "nature's machines," devoid of all thought and feeling. Some efforts are sometimes made, to be sure, to avoid and alleviate animal pain, but there is no law (at least not in the United States) that requires the use of anesthetic once an animal is in a scientific context; the decision to use or not to use anesthetic is left legally to the discretion of the investigator(s). And, of course, there is no law that protects nonhuman animals in laboratories against an untimely death. The proof of this (were proof to be required) is that although hundreds of millions of animals are killed in the name of science every year, no scientist has ever been convicted of violating any state or federal statute for killing an animal in the name of science.

The practical problem this customary practice in science poses for ethic-of-care feminism, I think, is that this practice seems to run directly counter to what an ethic of care, supplemented by appeals to logic, would sanction. For if humans are not "distinct from the animal and superior to it," then ethic-of-care feminism, when bolstered by consistency arguments, must demand that we take our moral equality with our animal kin seriously. And this in turn demands, I believe, that we not allow to be done to these animals "in the name of science" what we would not allow to be done to one of our own—in particular, one of those humans with whom we already have a caring, interpersonal relationship. Thus, since we most certainly would not permit a scientist to harm one of our friends, a spouse, a parent, or one of our children, treating them as a "tool" or "model" in the hope of benefiting others, I think we must conclude that science, if it were to be guided by the logically enriched moral principles of ethic-of-care feminism, would not permit this way of interacting with nonhuman animals either. In this sense, and for these reasons, ethic-of-care feminism must stand in favor of the total abolition of the harmful use of animals in science.

Whether this finding is true or not, it certainly seems provocative. Comparatively few scientists will welcome it (though the number of scientific antivivisectionists grows daily). And perhaps few feminists will welcome it (liberal feminists, for example, might claim that we "lower" the importance of being human if we argue for moral equality between humans and other animals). And yet this is the conclusion I think we should reach if (1) we accept the view that the dismantling of patriarchy requires that we attack it at its roots, if (2) part of these roots includes the view that humans are "distinct from the animal and superior to it," and if (3) a feminist ethic can allow a place for reason in ethics, especially in the form of consistency arguments, and thus can overcome the moral conservatism that seems to be indigenous to an ethic of care. All these points—(1) through (3)—are contentious, and none admits of simple proof or even simple reasonable defense. But having admitted, indeed, having insisted on, the problems we face in these troubled waters, I think we are right to conclude that just as nature is said to abhor a vacuum, so must an ethic-of-care feminism abhor vivisection.

"Politicizing" Science

Defenders of the status quo in science are unlikely to look with favor at the prospect of having ethic-of-care feminists in high places. One can even anticipate the charge that to force science to conform to the ethic of care, as this applies to non-human animals, would be to "politicize" this "apolitical" inquiry into truth. And this in turn engenders the specter of "outside interference" in the work of scientists. I think we know enough to recognize propaganda when we see it, so we will not be easily taken in by appeals to the "value-neutrality" of science or scientists. But the charge that we run the risk of "politicizing" science and the fear of "outside interference" deserve at least brief comment.

The plain fact is, science already is politicized. As the biologist Lynda Birke notes, "scientists are not at present free to pursue any line of inquiry in any way that they wish: public opinion and, to a much greater extent, sources of available funding, impose constraints upon what can be done. A woman wishing to do research relevant to feminist interests, for example, is quite likely to find it difficult to obtain funding, institutional support, laboratory space, or whatever. Yet a scientist doing military research of dubious benefit to humankind, is quite likely to obtain ample funding and facilities from defense budgets."[8]

What is true in the case of researching feminist topics is no less true in the case of developing alternatives to the use of animals in science. Consider the available support for developing such alternatives in the area of education. As the U.S. Congress's Office of Technology Report *Alternatives to Animal Use in Research, Testing, and Education* states, "in the long run, the most serious problem may be the lack of professional academic rewards for faculty members working in this area. Promotion, tenure, and salary increments are awarded predominantly for productivity in the research laboratory, not for efforts to develop innovative teaching techniques and materials."[9] Is science "apolitical"? Let us have an end to this breezy propaganda. The worry (some) scientists have is not that science, were it to be guided by feminist values, would become "politicized" (and thus "interfered with") but that the "politics" would be the wrong one. And that, of course, is an entirely different story, one that requires a careful assessment of the arguments at hand. Whatever their merit, we can at least agree with Lynda Birke when she writes that "the cry of 'interference!' raised when the issue of public accountability [of science] is brought up is of course nonsense, since science already is political, and in that sense, science already is 'interfered' with."[10]

Conclusion

I have argued that ethic-of-care feminism supports the abolitionist position in the case of the harmful use of animals in science. In claiming this, I reach a conclusion reached by some feminists—Frances Power Cobbe, for example, who was a major figure in both the suffragette and antivivisection movements in Victorian England, and Coral Lansbury, Carol Adams, and Roberta Kalechofsky among our contemporaries. Still, comparatively few of today's leading feminist thinkers and activists have joined Cobbe and the others in this conviction, which is all the more surprising given the initial role women played in the antivivisection movement, on the one hand, and, on the other hand, given the disproportionately large number of women, in comparison with the number of men, who are part of the estimated ten million people comprising the animal rights movement, broadly conceived.

Vivisection's nineteenth-century apologists were only too happy to heap scorn on Frances Power Cobbe and other women because of the excessive "sentimentality" that, they charged, characterized "this swarm of buzzing idlers," these "silly women led astray." What could explain why so many women, and so few men, would "bray persistent" against those noble scientists who labored on in their quest for nature's "hidden gifts of cure"?[11] The French physiologist Elie de Cyon has an answer: "Is it necessary to repeat that women—or rather, old maids—form the most numerous contingent of this group? Let my adversaries contradict me, if they can show me among the leaders of the agitation one girl, rich, beautiful, and beloved, or some young wife, who has found in her home the full satisfaction of her affections."[12] In caring for animals, in other words, women express their frustration at not being cared for enough themselves—by men, of course.

Elie de Cyon at least has the virtue of wearing his patriarchal prejudices on his sleeve, which is more than can be said of many. But the same kinds of prejudice toward women as those we find in Elie de Cyon are to be found today in the prevailing attitudes in science toward nonhuman animals. Or so I believe and have argued. The great pity is too few feminist thinkers and activists have seen the connection, too few are adding their voice to that of Alice Walker, who recognizes in the oppression of nonhuman animals in the lab the same pattern of oppression women face all over the world. Too few have seen this, and done this, up to now, that is.

Notes

I am especially indebted to Carol Adams for her many helpful criticisms of the original draft of this chapter. Whatever errors remain are solely my responsibility.

1. Mary Wollstonecraft, *A Vindication of the Rights of Women* (London: Dent, 1982), p. 15.

2. Val Plumwood, "Women, Humanity and Nature," *Radical Philosophy* 48 (1988): 22.

3. Amelia Bloomer, "Response to Mr. T. S. Arthur's 'Ruling a Wife,' " quoted in *Feminist Quotations: Voices of Rebels, Reformers, and Visionaries*, ed. Carol McPhee and Ann FitsGerald (New York: Crowell, 1979), p. 124.

4. Ariel Kay Salleh, "Contributing to the Critique of Political Epistemology," *Thesis Eleven* 8 (1984): 23–43.

5. Plumwood, "Women, Humanity and Nature," p. 26.

6. Marilyn French, *Beyond Power: Of Women, Men, and Morals* (New York: Ballantine Books, 1986), p. 341.

7. Carol Gilligan, *In a Different Voice: Psychological Theory and Women's Development* (Cambridge, Mass.: Harvard University Press, 1982).

8. Lynda Birke, *Women, Feminism, and Biology: The Feminist Challenge* (London: Routledge, Chapman & Hall, 1986), p. 159.

9. U.S. Congress, Office of Technology, *Alternatives to Animal Use in Research, Testing, and Education* (New York: Dekker, 1988), p. 214.

10. Birke, *Women, Feminism, and Biology*, p. 159.

11. These words are part of a poem entitled "Somnia Medici" that appeared in *Zoophilist* 5 (1 May 1885): 1. The author is unknown.

12. Elie de Cyon, "The Anti-Vivisectionist Agitation," *Contemporary Review* 43 (1883): 506.

2

Positive Freedom, Economic Justice, and the Redefinition of Democracy

Carol C. Gould

Recent theories of economic justice, most notably that of John Rawls, have generally focused on the question of just distribution of goods or wealth. Where they have focused on production, and not only distribution, such theories have generally operated with conceptions of property, specifically of private property, and of entitlement to the products of one's labor, as in Robert Nozick's *Anarchy, State, and Utopia*. Very few, if any, of these theories have given significant attention to the question of justice in the organization of the production process or to the distribution of powers and rights in this domain. In this chapter, I propose a conception of economic justice in which the right to participate in economic decision making in the production process, that is, workers' self-management, is understood as a requirement of justice. Although other theorists have argued for such workers' self-management, they have seen it as required not by justice but rather by such other values as meaningful work, property rights, and productive efficiency, or, most generally, by the value of democracy itself. I shall also consider a conception of market socialism that I take to be central to such a theory of economic democracy.

My interest in this chapter, however, is not only to provide a normative argument for workers' self-management but also to examine the more general normative foundations of democracy from which a principle of economic justice may be seen to follow. Thus, in this chapter, I propose a fundamental rethinking of democracy based on an analysis of the concepts of freedom and equality. I argue for a conception of justice in which it is understood as fundamentally involving equal positive freedom, that is, the equal right to the conditions of self-development, including enabling material and social conditions in addition to civil liberties and political rights. Here, I present a sketch of these philosophical foundations, focusing first on the conception of positive freedom, second on the argument for equality, and third on the derivation of rights to democratic participation in economic and social contexts. As part of this discussion, I consider the notions of common activity and common interests. In the rest of the chapter, I propose some basic features of a concrete model of self-management and market socialism, in which such principles of justice may come to be realized.

Inadequacies of Freedom as Constraint

I begin then with an interpretation of the concepts of freedom and equality that differs from the traditional conceptions in fundamental ways. On the whole, traditional political theory has taken freedom to mean the absence of external constraints. Thus, for example, Thomas Hobbes writes, "Liberty, or freedom, signifieth, properly, the absence of opposition; by opposition, I mean external impediments of motion." With respect to a person, liberty "consisteth in this, that he finds no stop, in doing what he has the will, desire or inclination to do."[1] A similar contemporary view is expressed by Isaiah Berlin, who writes, "I am normally said to be free to the degree to which no man or body of men interferes with my activity. Political liberty in this sense is simply the area within which a man can act unobstructed by others."[2]

Although this view captures an important aspect of what we understand by freedom, it leaves out two essential features of the concept. First, while it addresses the requirement that agents not be externally constrained in exercising their choices, it ignores the complementary requirement that the means necessary for realizing these choices need to be available. I argue that the social and material means for realizing purposes, or what I shall call the enabling conditions of action, are essential to freedom. Second, in its account of free choice, this view takes as its focus individual or isolated actions and leaves out of consideration the development over time of the agent or person through these actions and the realization of long-term purposes or plans. I argue that an adequate conception of freedom must relate the account of the exercise of free choice or the agent's actions to such a process of self-development. I will later specify the particular sense in which I use the term *self-development*. As will be seen, it differs sharply both from essentialist views of self-realization, such as Aristotle's, and from radical individualist conceptions of self-actualization or self-fulfillment.

The distinctions I propose here may be analyzed in terms of the distinction between negative and positive freedom that has been discussed in recent political theory.[3] The traditional view of freedom as freedom from external constraints may be understood as what has been called negative freedom, or "freedom from." On analysis, such a view presupposes free choice as an abstract capacity, which may be distinguished from the actual exercise of that capacity in making specific choices under given conditions. Thus, if person A chooses some particular course of action, c, we presuppose that A is capable of making choices in general and that A could instead have chosen some alternative course of action, c^1. In this context, negative freedom signifies that there is no external constraint on A's doing c if A so desires or wills. But negative freedom is not identical with the ability to make choices, for someone could freely make a choice to do *c* and yet be prevented by external impediments from carrying it out in action. Thus, this negative freedom has been characterized principally in terms of the absence of constraints or limitations on one's action, rather than in terms of the agent's incapacity to act or the unavailability of material means to carry out the desired action. Further, negative freedom has for the most part been understood in terms of freedom from constraints imposed by other persons, rather than in terms of external impediments of a natural sort. Negative liberty has accordingly been understood as applying primarily to contexts of political freedom, where it connotes the freedom of individuals from interference or control by the state or protection by the state of individuals from interference or harm by others.

In his classic discussion in "Two Concepts of Liberty," Isaiah Berlin introduces a sharp distinction between this form of freedom and positive freedom as the "freedom which consists in being one's own master," or of being "the instrument of my own, not of other men's, acts of will."[4] Berlin argues that this conception of positive freedom has led to the notion that "being one's own master" is identical with knowing what is best to do or what is rationally or ideally necessary. This is then associated with the idea of a higher self whose task it is to control or discipline the lower or irrational self, or the "passions." According to Berlin, this higher or "real" self is then identified with "something wider than the individual . . . as a 'social whole' of which the individual is an element or aspect . . . ; this entity is then identified as being the 'true' self which, by imposing its collective, or 'organic', single will upon its recalcitrant 'members', achieves its own, and therefore their 'higher' freedom."[5] Once a state is seen as embodying such a higher rationality, this is taken to justify coercing others for their own sake, since this is supposedly getting them to do what they would choose for themselves if they were fully rational.

On these grounds, Berlin rejects the notion of positive liberty as leading to totalitarian or coercive regimes and chooses instead negative liberty as what democratic states should be concerned with. I will consider this particular criticism of the concept of positive freedom later. Here I want to focus on the inadequacy of defining freedom as narrowly as Berlin does in terms of negative liberty alone. For, as I will argue, this view leaves out of account the positive conditions necessary for the realization of one's choices. Such conditions go beyond the mere absence of external constraint imposed by other people on one's actions.

Positive Freedom and Enabling Conditions

One may be free of external constraint by others and yet may not be free to realize one's chosen purposes because the necessary conditions or means are not available. Thus, for example, I am free to make the choice to travel to China, yet without the money to pay for the trip, I am lacking one of the conditions necessary to act on my choice. Thus, my freedom remains merely formal. Concrete freedom requires not only the absence of external constraint but also the availability of the objective conditions that are necessary if choices are to be effected. Such conditions may be characterized as *enabling conditions*, or positive conditions for action, in distinction from the *constraining conditions*, the absence of which defines negative freedom. Thus, for example, although there may be no legal or discriminatory barriers to prevent someone from entering a given profession or trade, one cannot make such a choice effectively if there are no jobs available. Thus, the availability of jobs is an enabling condition for making one's choice effective or for realizing one's purposes, even in the absence of interference by others in one's choice. The presence of such enabling, or positive, conditions is an essential constituent of what I am characterizing here as positive freedom, in the distinctive sense in which I am using it here.

I believe that Berlin is right to distinguish negative liberty from the conditions of its exercise and to insist that negative freedom is an important value in itself, as a protection against interference or coercion by others. Further, if the positive, or enabling, conditions were available but the freedom to make use of them was not protected, these conditions by themselves would be of no use in achieving one's purposes. However, with Macpherson, I think that Berlin is wrong to separate these conditions from the meaning of freedom, which, I would argue, in its full sense requires not only negative liberty as the absence of constraining conditions but also positive liberty as the presence of, or access to, enabling conditions.

Freedom and Self-Development

What sort of conception of freedom is it that has the three multiple requirements that I have posed here: capacity for choice and its exercise, absence of constraining conditions, and the availability of means? I may begin by briefly characterizing it as self-development, that is, as the freedom to develop oneself through one's actions, or as a process of realizing one's projects through activity in the course of which one forms one's character and develops capacities. This conception may be related to what has been called positive freedom, or "freedom to." Such concrete freedom goes beyond particular acts of choice or the fulfillment of short-term purposes and involves a process of the development of the person over time. Thus, this notion of freedom has a biographical or historical dimension in that it concerns the individual's self-transformation through the course of his or her life; and it also has a social dimension in that social relations and common purposes provide a fundamental context for such self-development. This conception, like that of negative freedom, also presupposes that people have the capacity for free choice and for acting to realize their purposes. However, the concept of positive freedom that I propose here emphasizes that in order to effect such choices concretely, a wide range of actual options need to be available to people, for only through such activity is self-development possible. Thus, this conception stresses the importance of the availability of the objective conditions—both material and social—without which the purposes could not be achieved. Among the material conditions are the means of subsistence as well as the means for labor and for leisure activity. The social conditions include cooperative forms of social interaction, reciprocal recognition of each one's free agency, and access to training, education, and various social institutions.

Yet the characterization of freedom in this sense as positive freedom does not mean that negative freedom is dispensable. Rather, as the absence of external constraint by other persons, negative freedom is also an essential presupposition for self-development. Thus, the guarantee of civil liberties and political rights is central in the view I propose.

In the view that I am proposing here, one may distinguish two aspects of freedom: first, what I would call freedom as capacity; and second, freedom as the exercise of this capacity in the form of self-development. Freedom as capacity refers to a fundamental characteristic of human action, namely, choosing among alternatives. Such choice is a constitutive feature of action, which is manifest in the intentionality or purposiveness of such action. Thus, what marks off human actions from mere bodily motions or causally determined responses is that they are consciously oriented to some end or goal, or express some intended meaning. Such actions are understood in terms of reasons people have for acting as they do, rather than in terms of physical or physiological causes.

Freedom as self-development, however, involves more than merely making choices or engaging in isolated actions. As suggested earlier, self-development connotes the process of concretely becoming the person one chooses to be through carrying out those actions that express one's own purposes and needs. This is not to say, however, that in such activity people realize some fixed, innate or pregiven nature, or that their capacities or characters unfold from preformed potentialities, but rather that they create or develop their natures through their activity.

In addition to this growth of capabilities, self-development also connotes the achievement of a person's projects or long-term goals. This aspect of self-development is likewise an expression of freedom in one of the main ordinary senses of that term, namely, that one is free in doing what one chooses to do and being able to achieve what one sets out to achieve. This is the sense of freedom as the power to effect one's purposes. However, as in the case of the cultivation of capacities, the serious sense of freedom in this context involves a process of realizing relatively long-term projects or goals and not simply realizing some ad hoc or disconnected desire. For it would be an inadequate sense of freedom if a person could only realize particular, disconnected intentions and desires and could not also attain such continuous and cumulative achievements.

It is not entailed here that such projects or goals are to be taken as narrowly individualistic or that the person's activity is to be understood as aiming at self-improvement. In fact, such projects may often be social, or common, ones. Further, projects, whether individual or social, normally involve not simply internal self-transformation in a subjective sense but also objective changes in the world in which the agents act to effect their purposes.

It may be the case that many actions that people engage in are not undertaken for the sake of their own purposes or needs but rather are imposed upon them by others. When a person is constrained, coerced, or manipulated to act on behalf of another's interests or aims, then it may be said that such actions do not contribute to the person's self-development. These are cases of domination by others, and the conception of freedom as self-development is incompatible with such domination. This is to be distinguished from those cases in which one person acts in another's interest without being coerced to do so.

What specifically counts as self-development obviously varies from one person to the next, since it is determined, in large part, by a person's choices. Thus, it is always an individual who is self-developing or free in this sense rather than social groups or society as a whole. Yet such individuals are not isolated but rather are social individuals. That is, they express who they are and become who they want to be in large part through their relations with others. Moreover, many of their actions are such that they are essentially social, that is, they are joint actions which could not be carried out by individuals alone. To this degree, the individual's own self-development depends on these social relations, and on the extent to which these others

are themselves self-developing. Here, however, I simply want
to emphasize the role of social relations in individuals' self-
development and therefore as a condition for their freedom.[6]
Later in the chapter, I will also consider the social category of
common activity as it bears on the argument for the extension
of democracy.

Social Aspects of Self-Development

Social relations enter into an individual's self-development in several ways. First, it is clear that many of the intentions
or purposes that individuals form are social in their origin.
Clearly, a person's conception of what is valuable or important
is affected by his or her process of socialization and by the
understandings and practices that constitute the social milieu.
Thus, there is a fund of language, knowledge, skills, and techniques that is socially transmitted and that serves as the frame-
work of individual activity. Second, relations with others in
joint or cooperative activity as well as social institutions—for
example, economic, political, or educational—provide objective conditions or means that are necessary for carrying out an
individual's aims. Thus, it is obvious that the contexts of work,
politics, family life, and social interaction more generally serve
as means for self-development. Third, beyond the individual
purposes or intentions that a person may have, there are social
or common purposes that are shared in by many individuals
and that a person may adopt as the aim of his or her actions.
Here, the self-development of an individual takes the form of
participation in such joint activity. Such collective activities as
collaboration on common work projects or participation in political movements are examples of these contexts of self-development. Fourth, an individual's self-development depends to
a large extent on the recognition by others of the individual as
free. In social life, this recognition by each individual of the
other's freedom is a relation of reciprocity, which stands in
contrast to the nonreciprocal social relations of domination and
exploitation. Fifth, social relations directly enter into an individual's self-development through the mutual support that

individuals may contribute to each other's self-development. Such mutuality may be defined as a social relation in which each person not only recognizes the other as free and equal but also takes the enhancement of the other's self-development as a conscious aim. Sixth, there is another sort of mutuality, which, unlike the one just discussed, operates only indirectly. It consists in the contribution that is made to an individual's self-development by all those individuals who, in the development of their own capacities, have enriched the range of possible human actions, intentions, skills, and practices. This cultivation of human capacities provides an individual with options or models for his or her own development. Thus, any high achievement—in the arts, in science, in sports, and so on—sets new standards for what is humanly possible.

Freedom as Self-Development: Criticisms and Replies

Several objections may be raised against the view of freedom as self-development that I have been presenting here. The first, and perhaps most obvious, criticism is that the concept of self-development is vacuous. That is, it seems to be applicable to every possible course of action that an individual may undertake. Thus, for example, rote performances, such as assembly-line work or household drudgery, or dead-end jobs, such as much secretarial work, would appear to count as cases of self-developing activity. Since it would not be reasonable to regard such activities in this way, and since the proposed concept of self-development does not appear to exclude them, the concept thus seems to be trivial or empty.

This objection would be correct and the concept would indeed be vacuous if it applied indiscriminately to any possible course of action or if it were to count the examples just given as instances of self-development. But, in fact, as I have already suggested, the courses of action that would count as self-developmental are only those that express the agent's own purposes and are not imposed upon them by others; that involve the growth of capacities or the enrichment of the individual's range of activity; and that serve to realize long-range projects, consciously undertaken. Such courses of action may also contribute to the development of an integrated character over time. What I have just proposed are clearly normative requirements that not every action or course of action meets. Thus, the cited examples of rote performances or dead-end jobs fail to meet these requirements and do not qualify as self-developmental. Such activities normally do not involve any growth of capacities by virtue of their repetitious quality, and thus they are taken to be stultifying. Similarly, they are most often under the control of others and thus are not expressions of the agents' own purposes or realizations of their own long-range projects. There may be aspects of such activities that in a larger context do contribute to an individual's self-development, as for example, one's relations with coworkers or earning a living in order to be personally independent, but taken in themselves, the cases cited would not generally be instances of self-development.

But, the objection may be raised, aren't the proposed normative requirements themselves so vague as to leave the concept almost as vacuous as it seemed to be before? Aren't such requirements as "the growth of capacities," "the agent's own purposes," and "long-term projects" too broad and general to articulate any useful conception of self-development? My answer to this objection may seem somewhat strange in that it appears to grant the objection: on the view of freedom that is proposed here, the normative requirements for what counts as self-development must of necessity remain broad and general. For any further specification would preempt the very freedom to choose one's own path of self-development that is the value at stake here. Thus, what specifically counts as self-development has to remain open to the self-definition or self-determination of individuals if it is to embody the value of freedom. Yet, since not every course of action satisfies even the broad requirements for self-development, as I have argued, there are limits as to what remains open to the self-determination of individuals if such determination is to count as self-developing. Thus, although the criterion is broad, it is not vacuous.

Nevertheless, one may object, if what specifically counts as self-development has to remain open to the self-determination of individuals, as suggested here, doesn't this leave self-development completely relativized to whatever any individual might choose? Isn't this, then, an asocial or even antisocial conception of freedom, and wouldn't it justify what are normally regarded as morally reprehensible courses of action, which are pernicious or destructive to others in the name of self-development? Against this objection, it may be recalled that human beings are here taken to be social individuals who realize their purposes through interaction with others, and thus self-development has social interaction as one of its conditions. This requirement provides some constraint on those courses of action that would be destructive of the possibilities of social interaction. For if one pursued some course of action that harmed or alienated others, then one would be denied the support and cooperation that these others could otherwise provide for one's own self-development. This is a variation of the Socratic argument in the *Apology* that harming others harms oneself. Yet it may be objected that this support could be obtained by coercing others to do what one required of them as the means for one's self-development. Such coercion, however, would be so preoccupying in order to be effective that the coercer would be diverted from the pursuit of his or her ends by concern with the means. A stronger normative requirement that would clearly exclude those actions that purport to be self-developing but that are destructive to others is proposed later as the central principle of this account of democratic theory, namely, the principle of equal rights to the conditions of self-development, or equal positive freedom. In terms of this principle, it will become clear that the self-development of each individual ought to be compatible with the equal right to self-development on the part of the others. Anticipating that the argument for this principle has been made, it follows that pernicious, destructive, and antisocial modes of action are normatively excluded. For it is just such actions that, by harming others, undercut or deny their possibilities for self-development and thus violate their equal right to such development.

However, it may be questioned whether people are in fact explicitly interested in so lofty-sounding an aim as self-development as the central goal of their activity rather than in such more commonsensical and concrete ends as making a living, enjoying themselves, getting an education, having friends, and so on—all of which are clearly purposeful activities. Such an objection misconstrues the conception of self-development that I have proposed by abstracting it from those modes of activity in which people pursue just such concrete ends. As I have suggested, freedom as self-development is precisely the process of realizing projects of one's own choosing and cultivating capacities in specific contexts, of which the particular ends cited above are examples. It is nothing over and above specific forms of activity, except in the special case where someone self-consciously takes self-development as an aim and sees these other activities as instrumental to it. But such a self-conscious articulation is not a requirement of the conception as I have presented it (no more than, say, a conscious awareness of Peano's axioms is necessary for doing arithmetic).

It is appropriate at this point to return to Isaiah Berlin's objection that the concept of positive freedom provides a justification for a coercive imposition by the state or the "social whole" of what is best for the individual. His claim is that the concept of positive freedom entails the idea that what is rationally necessary is embodied in a higher consciousness or self, which then becomes identified with the state. It is clear that this view has nothing to do with the concept of positive freedom as I have presented it and in fact is antithetical to it. First, the conception I have proposed rules out any specification of what is "best" or "rationally necessary" for individuals and refuses to suggest what they ought to choose. It is left to individuals to determine what is best for them. This is evident from the earlier discussion in which I criticized the view of freedom as "action in accordance with one's nature," because of its essentialism, as well as from my argument that the requirements for self-development must remain broad and general so as to accommodate the various choices of individuals. Further, my view rules out any paternalism in the name of some "higher good" inasmuch as my conception of positive freedom presupposes negative freedom, or freedom from external constraint on an individual's free choice, as its necessary condition. Second, the view I propose rejects the holism that Berlin alleges to be characteristic of the concept of positive freedom. Thus, I criticize the view that there is an overarching totality or organic whole, of which individuals are members or parts. Rather, I regard both the state and society as constituted entities, which have no existence apart from the individuals who make them up.

Beyond these differences between Berlin's view of positive freedom and my own, there is an additional criticism that may be made of Berlin's view. It is that the conception of the state as the legitimate interpreter of what is best or rationally necessary for individuals is not entailed by the original conception of positive freedom as being one's own master or being self-determining. It may rather be seen as an illegitimate transformation of the original idea (based on one historical interpretation of it), which Berlin employs to make his point. This criticism has been developed by C. B. Macpherson.[7]

Enabling Conditions and Prima Facie Rights

The concept of positive freedom as self-development presented so far in this chapter entails that people must have access to the material and social conditions for their activity if they are to realize their freedom. They have to be able to appropriate these conditions or lay claim to them in order to use them for their purposes. But this gives rise to the problem of adjudicating among these claims, in the contexts of social interaction in which the claims of one individual (or of a group of individuals) can be effective only if they are recognized by others. The question therefore arises: what principle or rule functions as a principle of distributive justice concerning the proper allocation of material and social resources? It thus addresses the validity of claims to these conditions, or the rights that people have to them. I shall argue here that justice should be interpreted as a principle of equal rights to the conditions of self-development, or equal positive freedom. The principle of equal rights is familiar in traditional liberal democratic theory. But there it appears as a principle of political equality, that is, equality in voting and in civil liberties and rights. Here, however, the principle of equal rights applies not only to such political contexts but to social and economic ones as well.

What, then, is the basis for this principle of equal rights to the conditions of self-development? It may be seen to be derived from the conception of freedom as capacity (the first sense of freedom) that I discussed earlier. It will be remembered that this is a conception of free choice as a basic feature of action, manifested in the intentionality or purposiveness of such actions. As such, it is a constitutive feature of human actions. Such free choice may therefore be said to be a universal feature of human agency that all human beings possess by virtue of being human. As I indicated earlier, this free choice is to be understood as the capacity for self-development, inasmuch as it is in the making of such choices that people realize their purposes and develop themselves. Although different individuals will of course exercise this capacity differently in their self-development, one may speak of it apart from such differences as an abstract capacity which all human beings have equally; that is, since it is defined as free choice, which is the bare capacity for self-development—however differently anyone may exercise it—there can be no difference in degree or kind in this capacity among individuals.

Since human beings are all equally agents in this way, and since their full or concrete freedom as self-development (the second sense of freedom) requires conditions, it follows prima facie that no agent has more of a right to these conditions than does any other. Therefore, I would argue that there is prima facie an equal right of access to the conditions of self-development. The basis for arguing that no individual has more of a right to the conditions than any other is, in the first place, that no distinctions can be made among individuals with respect to their agency or their bare capacity for self-development. A possible counterargument to this view is that agents have differing capacities for freedom, and that their rights should therefore be commensurate with their capacities. Against this, I would argue that a distinction needs to be drawn between the general capacity for self-development and the particular talents and abilities in which individuals may clearly differ. Though it may make sense to claim that one individual has a greater capacity for musical or athletic development than another, this must be distinguished from the general capacity for self-development as such, which, I argue, provides no basis for discrimination among individuals.

I would argue that every person, being equally an agent, has an equal claim to the conditions that are required for the exercise of this agency in self-development. This follows from the fact that the mere possession of the capacity for self-development is not sufficient for the realization of freedom. Rather, this capacity has to be exercised in concrete actions, which require material and social conditions. The normative imperative to realize one's freedom in this way is, as I argued earlier, posited in the very nature of human activity itself. But without the availability of the conditions for such self-development, the imperative remains empty. Thus, the force of any individual's claim to the conditions derives in part from this imperative.[8] And because this imperative holds equally for each agent, their claims to the conditions are also prima facie equal.

However, it may be objected that such equal claims do not yet amount to equal *rights* to the conditions. Again, the mere fact that someone needs or desires a condition for their self-development, or that it is a value for them, does not imply that they have a right to it. To answer this objection, one would have to show how rights are integral to, or may be derived from, the conception of freedom as self-development. If the premises are true that the concrete freedom of human beings is an activity of self-development and further that free choice as a capacity for such self-development is what characterizes human beings as human, then it follows that the recognition of someone as a human being entails at the very least a recognition of that person as having this capacity (whether it is exercised or not). But, as I have argued, individuals cannot exercise this freedom of choice as a capacity for self-development without the requisite conditions; that is, this freedom remains abstract and unrealized unless the concrete means for the activity of self-development are available. Therefore, to recognize persons as free to develop themselves but not to recognize the validity of their (equal) claims to the conditions of this freedom would be empty. It would be a failure to recognize what is entailed by the concept of free choice as a capacity for self-development. To claim to understand A and also that A entails B and then to refuse to conclude therefore *that-B* would be to fail to be rationally consistent where A is the (compound) proposition that free choice is a capacity for self-development and that there is a normative imperative for its exercise and that such exercise requires conditions, and where this entails B, that there is a normatively valid claim to these conditions. Therefore, we may conclude that since the availability of conditions is an essential part of what constitutes the meaning of the freedom of individuals to develop themselves, the recognition of this freedom entails a recognition of the validity of their claims to the conditions for self-development. But a valid claim is what we mean by a right. It follows that the recognition of human beings as human entails the recognition of their rights to the conditions of their freedom.

But there is one more essential step to this argument. Freedom as free choice, or the capacity for self-development, is, as I argued earlier, equally possessed by all persons by virtue of their being human. Therefore, they may be said, prima facie, equally to have valid claims on the conditions. That is, all individuals have prima facie equal rights to the conditions of self-development. This is the principle of equality that I would propose as commensurate with the conception of freedom presented earlier. It may be characterized as the principle of equal positive freedom.

Equal rights to the conditions of self-development require a certain form of social relations if they are to be realized, for as I argued earlier in this chapter, it would require the recognition by each individual of the equal freedom of the others. Such a relation is therefore one of reciprocal recognition of their equal agency. This relation of reciprocity, which may be seen as one of the social conditions for self-development, needs further analysis, but there is not space to discuss it here.[9]

Common Activity

Another form of social relations that has import for the conception of freedom as self-development and also for the form and scope of democratic decision making is what we may call common, or joint, activity, namely, activity in which a group of individuals acts to realize a common, or shared, aim.

Common activity may be defined as activity in which a number of individuals join together to effect a given end. This end, or aim, may be a shared end in the sense that they have all freely chosen it together, or it may be shared only in the weaker sense that they all cooperate to effect an end that was set for them by someone else or even imposed on them from without and that they have not chosen. Further, such common activity may be aimed either at the common good of all those who participate in it or at some private or external good. Insofar as it is aimed at the common good, this end may be chosen by the members of the group themselves, who jointly determine it; or it may be chosen for them, or on their behalf, by someone else (on the presumption that they are not competent to choose it for themselves or on the paternalistic premise that someone else knows better what is best for them). However, it is only where they choose for themselves what the end of the activity shall be and what the good is that it is intended to serve that we shall speak of genuinely common activity in the strong sense, as distinguished from common activity in general.

Common activity obviously contrasts with individual activity undertaken for individual ends and also from any mere aggregation of individual activities in pursuit of such ends. Such common activity essentially involves the cooperation and coordination of many individuals in the realization of their joint projects or purposes. Though there may be ends that would be achieved either by individual or by common activity, there nevertheless is a large class of projects that can only be realized through such cooperation. Moreover, such socially achievable projects constitute an essential part of what human beings require for meeting their life needs and for their self-development. Thus, for example, any branch of economic production requires such socially organized forms of activity, and so too does any political system. Further, as suggested earlier, the experience of participating in, and cooperating with, others in common tasks serves as one of the conditions of individual self-development. In such contexts, individuals have the opportunity to exercise and develop their social, moral, and intellectual capacities.

The question might be raised concerning whether such common activity subordinates the individual to the group as a whole and delimits his or her freedom and initiative. Both the historical and the recent experience of the supervenience of the authority and power of totalities over individuals make this a sharp issue for any theory of democracy in which common activity or sociality plays an important role. The relation of the group to the individual in common activity would appear to be holistic in nature if the choice of the ends of the group's activity were imposed upon its members by some external power or authority over which they had no control, or if the members themselves, having originally determined their common purpose and their rules of operation, so fetishize or reify the group as to relinquish all future power of decision. Totalitarian states or religious cults easily come to mind as egregious examples of such supervening authority and power of the group over its members, and many lesser examples may be cited as well. However, even in such cases, the individuals retain the capacity to choose to reject the external authority or to dissolve the group. Such a choice may not be a rationally feasible one under all conditions and may require further the creation of the conditions for realizing such changes.

Of course, the possibility of such a holistic interpretation of common activity or of groups does not arise in the case of what I have characterized as genuinely common activity. For here the choice of a shared or a common good is always determined by the individuals who constitute the group and who recognize each other reciprocally as free and equal members of it. There is thus no possibility of a supervenient or external authority that can impose its will upon the group. However, there remains the danger that the members of such a freely constituted group may reify the group's own authority and relinquish all participation in decisions about its aims and activities. The holistic interpretation of such a reified authority would simply reflect this same misconception, mistaking the apparent reified authority for the real authority of the individuals who constitute the group.

Redefining Democracy

The principle of democracy to be established here is the following: every person who engages in a common activity with others has an equal right to participate in making decisions concerning such activity. This right to participate applies not only to the domain of politics but to social and economic activities as well. The scope of such decision making includes both the determination of the ends of the common activity and the ways in which it is to be carried out. The argument for this principle of democracy begins with the proposition argued for earlier, that freedom as self-development is grounded in agency, or the capacity for choice, and that it can be attained only through activities that individuals freely determine.

If individuals have an equal right to determine their own actions, and further, if engaging in common activity is one of the necessary conditions for an individual's self-development (where self-development, and not agency alone, is the meaning of concrete freedom), then it follows that there is an equal right to participate in determining the course of such common activity. For if an individual were to take part in common activity without having any role in making decisions about it and under the direction of another, then this would not be an activity of self-development, since such self-development requires determining the course of one's activity. It is only in this sense that common activity can be a condition for self-development. And since there is an equal right to the conditions of self-development, it follows that there is an equal right to make decisions about such common activity.

Clearly, since the form of such common activity differs from individual activity, in which one makes decisions about one's own actions independently of others, the nature of decision making in common activity must also differ. It cannot simply be the aggregate of individuals' decisions about their own separate actions. Rather, as joint activity defined by common purposes, it requires a form of participation in the common decisions that bind all the members of the group. Thus, its appropriate form is codetermination, or shared decision making among equals. The general conclusion of this argument, as stated above, is therefore that all individuals who are engaged in a common activity have an equal right to participate in the decisions concerning it. But this is to say that, in principle, there is a normative requirement for the right to democratic participation in decision making in all the contexts of common activity. Therefore, this argues for the extension of democracy beyond the context of political life alone to decision making in economic and social contexts as well, for so much of common activity takes place in these contexts.

The proposed extension of democracy beyond the political sphere to the arenas of economic and social life has some important implications for changes in the organizations and institutional structures in these domains. As will be seen, perhaps the most important implication is the requirement for workers' self-management, as the institutional form of the extension of democracy to the workplace or the firm. I also argue that democracy should apply as well to decision making concerning the broader contexts of economic policy. Further, I would argue that it should extend to forms of common activity in social life, such as educational and cultural institutions and local community organizations.

A theory of economic justice concerns the principles that ought to govern the distribution of rights, powers, and goods within the economic domain. The main principle of justice that I proposed earlier is that of equal positive freedom, defined as prima facie equal rights to the (social and material) conditions of self-development. Interpreted as a principle of economic justice, it would require equal rights of access to the economic conditions of one's self-development. It may be noted, though without further discussion here, that this prima facie equality is qualified by some permissible inequalities. Furthermore, I propose that economic justice also entails a principle of reciprocity, in addition to the fundamental principle of equal rights. If economic justice is understood in terms of this principle of equal rights to the conditions of self-development, then it is clear that it pertains not only to the distribution of material goods but also to the distribution of rights and powers that are involved in economic production, since these rights and powers are among the social conditions necessary for agency. Central among such rights is the right to participate in decisions or choices concerning the productive activities in which one engages jointly with others.

Workers' Self-Management

Such workers' self-management is therefore analogous to democracy in political life, in which the equal right to participate in decisions concerning common actions is recognized. The argument is similar in both cases, namely, that free agents have a right of self-determination, or self-rule, which therefore implies an equal right of codetermination concerning all common activities in which they engage, whether political or economic. In the case of economic democracy, I would define the locus of participation in decision making more narrowly as, in the first instance, the basic unit of production. In most cases this would be the firm. The argument for this restriction is that the right of codetermination belongs to those who are themselves agents in this activity, that is, who are engaged in a common project. Thus, I am not proposing that all those who are affected by an economic activity have a right to participate in decisions about production, but rather that it is the producers themselves that principally have this right. This formulation avoids the objection that has been raised against proposals for economic democracy to the effect that there is no way of demarcating who is or who is not affected by economic decisions. Thus, it is argued that ultimately everyone is affected and, therefore, that such participation in economic decision making is unworkable and meaningless. On my proposal, the locus of decision making in matters of production is principally defined as the firm, and participation is in the first instance delimited to those who are actively engaged in the firm. Therefore, the firm retains relative autonomy as the principal locus of participation in economic decision making.[10]

Workers' self-management in this model would mean that the workers in a firm would have the right to jointly decide on questions of the planning and organization of production or the provision of services, including what to produce or what services to provide, as well as rates of production, allocation of work, working hours, work discipline, and so on. They would also have the right to determine jointly how the firm's income is to be distributed, for example, how much of it is to be plowed back into the firm itself, how much is to be distributed in wages, and how these wages are to be divided among themselves. They would also control the decisions concerning sales and marketing of the product or service. However, this workers' self-management surely does not require that all the workers participate in every decision concerning all aspects of production and sale of their products. In any large firm, one would expect that they would delegate various functions to directors and managers whom they appoint. However, in this model, ultimate authority and decision-making power remains with all those who work in the firm.

It is clear, then, that workers' self-management as it is described here involves more than worker participation in the management decisions of privately owned corporations. Rather, it is understood as worker control, that is, as involving property rights of ownership, as well as management rights. In this way, this view entails a conception of social, or cooperative, ownership of the means of production by the participating workers in a firm.[11] I give the argument for this conception of property elsewhere.[12]

However, economic production involves more than the single firm as its unit. It typically involves complex interactions among many firms through a market or other means of exchange (for example, in the acquisition or sale of raw or processed materials for production, of tools, transportation, and warehousing, and, again, of credit facilities, and so on). In such complex economic interactions, decisions are made through the medium of the market itself, where the joint decisions of the members of each firm come into play with respect to each other. Insofar as the market permits a free agreement based on the decisions of worker-controlled firms, it is compatible with such economic democracy. In the model proposed here, then, firms are free to buy and sell to other firms, to institutions, or to individual consumers. The market is the focus for such exchanges and therefore adjusts supply and demand and influences the setting of prices. However, this model would generally exclude the market between capital and labor, since the wages would be determined in the process of self-management, by the workers' own allocation among themselves of the net revenue of the firm.

Yet there is a domain of economic decision making that involves questions of social policy, regional or national economic planning and investment, taxation, and welfare. Since such questions involve the most general conditions for the economic activity of all those who are participants in the common economic life, for example, of a nation, the right to participate in decision making concerning such matters properly extends to all those who are involved. Such participation should be direct where possible but may of course proceed through representation where necessary. Furthermore, it may be part of the political processes of decision making in a democratic government. In the context of such regional or national economic policy, one may propose that there should be market-regulatory and planning, or investment, commissions, which are democratically representative. These would aim at serving general social interests—for example, by regulating abuses of the market system, by some long-range planning to meet expected social needs, and by fostering innovation.

By including all the members of the firm as part of the worker self-management structure, I am suggesting that this would encompass those workers who are now regarded as managerial personnel, such as supervisors, engineers, and so on. Further, since this model takes the firm to be the shared property of the workers, "self-management" here encompasses not only managerial but also ownership functions. This is not to say, however, that there is necessarily a carryover into the worker-controlled firm of exactly the same managerial or ownership functions that are found in present privately owned firms. For the social relations between workers and managers and between workers and employers that are characteristic of the present form and that often represent conflicts of economic and social interest would no longer obtain, though new sorts of difficulties in the social relations among workers in self-managed firms may well arise.

Such workers' self-management does not entail that all the workers decide on every feature of the production and sale of their products. They may well decide to appoint directors or managers of various aspects of the firm's activities. However, such delegation of powers and functions rests entirely upon the democratic decision of all those who work in the firm. This democratic decision making should involve direct and immediate participation up through as many levels of the firm's activities as is feasible. What is intended here, of course, is that all those who work in the firm have an equal *right* to participate in decisions, not that they are required or obliged to do so.

Advantages of Socialist Market

Another major feature of the proposed economic structure is the market. Firms are free to buy and sell to other firms, to institutions, or to individual consumers. The market therefore determines prices and serves as an instrument for adjusting supply and demand. Thus, the market functions as the focus for the exchange of commodities. However, unlike the capitalist market, what is excluded here is the market between capital and labor. Rather, the workers' incomes are determined by their own division of the net revenue of the firm among themselves.

In terms of the values and principles discussed earlier, the virtues of such a market scheme are three. First, it preserves the freedom of workers to determine what to produce and the freedom of consumers to determine what, and from whom, to buy. In the ideal market, the firms relate to each other and to individual consumers as free and equal exchangers. Second, the market is an efficient means of reflecting the needs and wants of consumers and of adjusting supply to meet the effective demand. Third, the market fosters variety in what is produced because it expresses the multiplicity of wants and it leaves producers free to satisfy them. In all these respects, the market is superior to a centralized planning scheme in which decisions are made from the top down, as they are in many existing socialist economies. Such centralized planning removes the autonomy of the workers in determining production, is often inefficient, and fails to provide variety because the planning bureaucracies tend to be insensitive to differentiated demands and cumbersome in adjusting supply to demand. However, in claiming that the market is suited to realize the principles, I do not mean to imply that it is the only system that could satisfy these principles. But the market form is already available and well-developed and requires no third party to intervene between producers and consumers or to validate their choices.

Against this, it may be argued that the introduction of a market economy—even in the democratic contexts of worker self-management, with its egalitarian tendencies—would simply reproduce the worst features of existing corporate market economies, namely, class polarization with gross inequalities of wealth; domination over, and exploitation of, labor; and the relentless pursuit of profit without any consideration of social need. But this argument, which attributes these ills to the systemic tendencies of market economies as such, seems specious. For it is not the market as such that produces these outcomes but rather the social relations of property, in which control by some over the conditions of productive activity of others leads to domination and exploitation. This requires a market in labor, and the model here explicitly excludes that. Further, the democratic structure of self-management proposed here would eliminate such property-based power of some over others.

There are also other ways in which the economic model

proposed here could avoid some of these consequences of present market economies. The application of the principles described earlier could be expected to mitigate some of the extreme inequities that an unbridled market economy may produce. Further, the habits of cooperation induced by the participatory practices of self-managing firms would likely generate a more cooperative and less cutthroat ambience for market competition as well. Again, since there would be no labor market, workers would not be totally dependent on the market as wage-labor, since they would also share in the proprietorship of the firms of which they are members (though it is true that these firms would be engaged in market competition with others, and the workers' livelihood would fluctuate with market conditions in this sense). The unrestricted pursuit of profit without regard for social need would have to be regulated (see the final section of this chapter), but among worker self-managed firms, the pursuit of profit may be justified insofar as it produces the goods and provides the widest conditions of material well-being and choice for the self-development of the individuals of a society.

There are other problems arising in a market-oriented economy that have been widely observed and criticized but that do not stem from the nature of the market economy itself and are rather attributed to abuses of it. These would have to be considered in a worker self-managed economy as well, insofar as they may still arise. These include attempts to control the market by means of collusion among firms or by monopolistic practices, such as price-fixing; attempts to manipulate consumer demand by deceptive advertising; and the pursuit of profit without regard to larger social needs or public welfare, for example, by disregarding consumer safety or environmental hazards. (However, it may be suggested that worker self-managed firms would be less likely than traditional capitalist firms to permit violations of the occupational safety of the workers themselves in the pursuit of profits.) In the proposed model, problems arising from market practices would be the province of market-regulatory and planning commissions.

Planning and Market-Regulatory Commissions

Such commissions constitute an important feature of the proposed economic structure. The planning commissions would affect the direction of production in the economy indirectly, by making funds available for new investment to existing or prospective worker-managed firms. The commissions would derive these funds from taxation of the social capital of firms. They would operate regionally where possible, though some national planning would be necessary.

These commissions would be political bodies in the sense that they would be made up of elected representatives of the people. They would not be chosen as representatives of the workers in the firms, but rather by workers in general, in their capacity as citizens, who would presumably be in a better position to make decisions in the interests of society as a whole. The unit to be represented on the planning commission would, therefore, be a political unit at the most local level possible, rather than an economic unit (for example, a firm or an industry).

The market-regulatory commissions would function to see to it that the market is free of abuses, such as price-fixing, monopolistic practices, violations of contract, or deceptive advertising or merchandising practices. These commissions are intended not to control the market but to permit it to operate fairly and effectively. Like the planning commissions, the market-regulatory commissions would also be democratically elected entities representing the public.

Both the planning commissions and the market-regulatory commissions are necessary to correct malfunctions of the economy and to help it to meet social needs. Thus, although worker self-managed firms and the market are seen as the principal moving force and adjustment mechanism, respectively, of the economy, nonetheless, they cannot be expected to meet all the needs optimally or may sometimes meet them in a haphazard or distorted way. The commissions, in representing the general social interest, are thus balancing and corrective mechanisms and can also foster innovation to meet important social and economic needs.

What I have dealt with in this chapter, then, are the normative foundations of democracy. These foundations are, first, freedom, but not simply freedom from constraint; rather, freedom as an activity and, in particular, as an activity of self-development involving choice and requiring external material and social conditions. Second, this very concept of freedom entails an equal right of all agents to the conditions of their self-development and, therefore, a principle of equality that I characterized as equal positive freedom. Finally, the practical context of such free activity by equal agents is an activity in which they are essentially and internally related to each other as social individuals or as individuals-in-relations, and that common activity in pursuit of joint interests is therefore crucial for their self-development. I have tried to show how, on these normative foundations, one needs to redefine democracy so that the right to participate in decision making extends beyond the domain of political democracy or electoral politics to all contexts of common activity, including the social, the economic, and the cultural. And specifically, it has been emphasized that in the economic sphere, justice as the application of the principle of equal positive freedom in this domain requires equal rights to participate in decisions in the firm for all those working in it, that is, workers' self-management. The burden of my argument has been less on the empirical details than on the philosophical discussion of norms, their justification, and the consequences for social and political life that flow from them. In redefining democracy in this way, the intent is not to close the discussion on these issues but rather to open it.

Notes

1. Thomas Hobbes, *Leviathan* (New York: Collier Books, 1962), p. 159.
2. Isaiah Berlin, "Two Concepts of Liberty," in *Four Essays on Liberty* (Oxford: Oxford University Press, 1970), p. 122.

3. The distinction between negative and positive liberty is explicitly drawn by Isaiah Berlin in his "Two Concepts of Liberty." This distinction is also discussed by Stanley I. Benn and Richard Stanley Peters in *The Principles of Political Thought* (New York: The Free Press, 1965); Gerald MacCallum in "Negative and Positive Freedom," *Philosophical Review* 76, no. 3 (July 1967); and Joel Feinberg in *Social Philosophy* (Englewood Cliffs, N.J.: Prentice-Hall, 1973). These treatments are for the most part critical of the concept of positive liberty. Virginia Held's *Rights and Goods* (New York: The Free Press, 1984), pp. 124–38, also contains an interesting discussion of this distinction. Lawrence Crocker's *Positive Liberty* (The Hague: Martinus Nijhoff, 1980) contains a full consideration of the distinction and a defense of the concept of positive liberty. The classical criticism of Berlin's view and a development of the concept of positive liberty is in Crawford Brough Macpherson's *Democratic Theory: Essays in Retrieval* (Oxford: Oxford University Press, 1973).

4. Berlin, "Two Concepts of Liberty," p. 131.

5. Berlin, "Two Concepts of Liberty," p. 132.

6. See Carol C. Gould, *Rethinking Democracy: Freedom and Social Cooperation in Politics, Economy, and Society* (New York: Cambridge University Press, 1988), chapters 2 and 3, pp. 92–132.

7. Macpherson, "Berlin's Division of Liberty," in *Democratic Theory*, pp. 95–119.

8. I say "in part" here because the claim that an individual has to the conditions of his or her own self-development also derives in part from the social role that each individual plays with respect to others in constituting an aspect of the social conditions that are required for each one's self-development. An individual's claim thus derives in part from the recognition by other individuals of their need for this individual, i.e., from their mutual recognition of their interdependence.

9. See Gould, *Rethinking Democracy*, pp. 133–59.

10. It may be argued that those outside the firm have an indirect voice in production decisions insofar as they constitute the market for the firm's products and thus set the conditions for the profitability of the firm. However, the market does not make decisions about production but only provides some of the information on the basis of which those engaged in the firm would make their decisions.

11. One possible objection to the idea of workers' self-management is that it substitutes a mere show of participation in decision making for a real change in the economic power structure, since it leaves ownership and hence ultimate control over the conditions of

activity in the hands of others. This objection has been raised with respect to worker participation in schemes at lower levels of management decision making or in "quality-of-life" circles in industry, and also with respect to collaboration between labor and business in such institutionalized contexts as "codetermination" (*Mitbestimmung*) in some West European cases. Clearly, my view is not subject to this criticism, for as indicated, I take workers' self-management to include worker control. At the same time, the argument I develop here is not incompatible with degrees of worker self-management short of worker control, insofar as these represent increases in democratic participation. For a discussion of the details of my model of self-management, see chapter 9, in Gould, *Rethinking Democracy*, pp. 247–61.

   12. See Gould, *Rethinking Democracy*, pp. 171–89.

3

Prejudice and Equal Treatment

James Rachels

People ought to be treated equally. Often they are not. Among the important reasons is prejudice. Social policies should be devised with this in mind. Such policies should contain provisions to insure that people are given equal treatment, insofar as this is possible, despite the fact that those who administer the policies may be prejudiced against them.

Human Differences

"All men," said Thomas Jefferson, "are created equal." Although he owned slaves, Jefferson knew that slavery is not compatible with such sentiments, and he wanted to write a condemnation of slavery into the Declaration of Independence. But, yielding to political pressures, he did not, showing how much easier it is to proclaim an ideal than to put it into practice.

In the case of equality, however, it is not easy even to proclaim the ideal in a clear and coherent manner. Exactly what is meant by saying that all persons are equal? Taken as a description of human beings, the claim that all are equal is plainly false. People differ in intelligence, beauty, talent, moral virtue, and physical strength; in fact, they differ in virtually every characteristic that might be thought important.

Elitists—if I may use that somewhat misleading term—have believed that these differences are the work of nature itself and have concluded that some of us are, by nature, better than others. From ancient times social inequality has been defended as the natural outcome of such differences. Plato, in the *Republic*, argued that rigid social classes are necessary because people are by nature suited to different tasks: some to labor, some to soldier, and some to rule. In the *Politics* the first task Aristotle sets himself is to explain how the "component parts" of the state differ from one another, that is, how men differ from women, masters from slaves, and so on. It turns out, in his analysis, that the free man deserves his exalted status because of his superior intelligence. But Aristotle quickly adds that this does not mean females and slaves, both deficient in intelligence, belong together in the same class, for there are differences between them also. It is depressing to see perhaps the greatest mind in the history of Western civilization going on and on in this vein.

Egalitarians have countered by insisting that, contrary to appearances, all people really are equal. Elitism is an ancient view. Egalitarianism is, by contrast, more recent. In the eighteenth century, there was a popular theory of human nature according to which our differences are produced entirely by environment and experience; at birth, it was said, we are all alike. (Jefferson's proclamation reflects this: he says that all men are *created* equal.) Now of course the *philosophers* did not mean to deny that there are natural physical differences between people. The fact that one person is red-headed while another is blond, or that one is tall while another is short, was conceded to be a matter of natural endowment. But a person's psychological characteristics were viewed differently. In such matters as intelligence, talent, and character, there were thought to be no significant natural differences.

This view was most clearly expressed by Helvétius in his

Treatise on Man, first published in 1773. "I consider intelligence, genius, and virtue," he said, "as the products of learning." As concerns intelligence, "everyone is equally able to comprehend the highest truths." If some do not, it is either because they do not desire to do so or because they are handicapped by social position. But these two causes really reduce to one, for the desire to learn is itself controlled by "the difference of situations" in which people find themselves. In sum, Helvétius declared that our minds are "perfect machines" that need only to be properly set in motion; then any of us will be the intellectual and moral equal of anyone else.[1]

This sort of view has provided support for egalitarian political movements down to the present day. After all, if people are at the outset so equal, and if the environment determines so much, why shouldn't the environment be arranged to provide maximum opportunities for everyone? In this view, it is not the fault of the individual or of nature if someone grows up stupid, lazy, or mean. It is society's fault—society is structured so that some have the chance to develop their potentials while others do not. This is obviously unfair. Therefore, society ought to be restructured so that everyone is able to develop those personal qualities that in the past have been possible for only a few. Trotsky, in his book *Literature and Revolution*, summed up the egalitarian expectation. Getting a bit carried away, he predicted that after conventional barriers to achievement have been removed, "man will become immeasurably stronger, wiser, and subtler; his body will become more harmonized, his movements more rhythmic, his voice more musical. The forms of life will become dynamically dramatic. The average human type will rise to the heights of an Aristotle, a Goethe, or a Marx."[2]

The egalitarian theory of human nature is just what we should expect from the endlessly optimistic philosophers of the Enlightenment and from their liberal descendants. It is hard to think of a more flattering view of ourselves. In this view, even the least of us is potentially a magnificent being. But the very appeal of such a view should be a warning. We may want to believe it, but is it true?

The egalitarian theory of human nature was, as I have said, a reaction against elitist theories of natural superiority. But, equally importantly, it was also inspired by the empiricist philosophy of mind fashionable in the eighteenth century. According to Locke, Hume, and others, the mind is at birth a "blank tablet" containing no information at all. A person has no knowledge or understanding as part of his or her "original equipment"; those things come only with experience. Thus, the abstract epistemological theories of the philosophers seemed to support the egalitarian theory needed to attack the old systems of class and privilege: given the "blank tablet" view of the infant's mind, it seemed natural to conclude that differences between adults are due only to experience and education. However, the appearance of support was only an illusion, for the empiricist theory of mind did not really entail human equality, even in the original status of infants. It may be that we are equal at birth in that none of us possesses any knowledge or understanding. But we may nevertheless be quite unequal in that some of us are endowed with a greater capacity for acquiring them.

It is, in fact, tolerably clear that some people are born with a greater capacity for learning than others. Compare yourself with a person with Down's syndrome. It is clear that you were better endowed at birth than that unfortunate person. Of course, an egalitarian might object to this comparison on the grounds that Down's individuals are not "normal," and the theory of human nature might then be reformulated to say only that all nondefective humans have equal native endowments. And of course the amendment may be interpreted in a way that avoids circularity.

But even with this modification, the egalitarian theory of human nature still asks us to believe something quite incredible. We are asked to believe that Chopin, who was already composing sonatas at age seven, had no special gift not also possessed by millions of other children whose piano lessons produce only mediocre renditions of simple melodies. And that Ramanujan, the Indian who reproduced much of mathematical science without realizing it had been done before, had no more natural mathematical ability than you or I. And that Sammy Reshevsky, whose chess exploits were legendary while he was still a child, had nothing in him not shared by everyone else.

If we knew more about the physical basis of behavior—the brain, the chemistry of the central nervous system, and so on—we would be in a better position to make a definitive assessment of the egalitarian theory. It is conceivable, for example, that at birth every normal human has exactly the same brain and associated chemistry. This would be a powerful argument for sameness of potential. But there is little reason to think this is so and much reason to doubt it. Although our knowledge of such matters is far from complete, the situation seems to be that, while our "original equipment" is substantially similar, there are nevertheless minute differences that could very well be significant.

Of course, as incredible as it would be, the egalitarian theory of human nature might be true. There might be environmentalist explanations, unknown to us, that would account for Chopin and Ramanujan and Reshevsky—as well as for Mozart, Newton, Hume, Jane Austen, and Einstein—without assuming their native endowments to be in any way superior to our own. But until such explanations are found, this form of egalitarianism must be regarded as little more than a pious hope. Without strong supporting evidence, which is at present unavailable, it is unbelievable. We need not go so far as to believe with Aristotle that some people are natural slaves to realize that, as a working hypothesis, we must assume that people come with a variety of natural endowments.

The Principle of Equality

If the idea of equality is to be at all plausible, then, it cannot be interpreted as a view about the facts, as describing how human beings are. Instead, it must be understood as a principle governing how people are to be treated—as a moral rule saying, roughly, that people are to be treated as equals.

But there are problems with this too. If people are not in

fact equals, why should they be treated as such? This simple challenge has caused some skeptical philosophers to abandon the idea of equality altogether, as a misguided ideal. The skeptics have a point, for surely we do not want people always to be treated alike. A doctor, for example, should not always prescribe the same treatment for all patients, regardless of what ails them. It would be a grisly joke always to prescribe penicillin on the "egalitarian" grounds that this treats everyone alike. And should the admissions committee of a law school be required to admit all applicants (or reject them all) because this treats them all as "equals"? Obviously not. Because all applicants are not equals, it makes no sense to treat them as though they are.

We must formulate our principle in such a way as to take this point into account. The basic idea that must be worked into the principle is that treating people differently is not objectionable if there is a relevant difference between them that justifies a difference in treatment. Thus, if one patient has an infection treatable by penicillin, while another patient has no such condition, it is permissible to give one but not the other an injection of that drug. The difference between the patients justifies the difference in treatment. But if there were no such difference between them—if both had exactly the same medical problem—there should be no difference in the treatment prescribed. Similarly, if one law school applicant has a good college record and has scored well on the qualifying examinations while another applicant has a poor record, it is permissible to admit one but not the other. Again the difference between the people involved justifies the difference in treatment.

This means that equality is not to be understood as an absolute demand always to treat people in the same way, no matter what. It is, instead, a presumption in favor of treating individuals in the same way—a presumption that may be set aside when, but only when, there is a specific justification for doing so. The shift from thinking of equality as an absolute demand to thinking of it as a presumption does not emasculate the ideal. Equality has this in common with other moral principles. The rule against causing pain, for example, has a central place in our morality; yet it does not impose an absolute requirement. (It is sometimes permissible to cause pain, if there is a sufficient justification for doing so.) If the presumptive nature of the equality principle were a flaw, then virtually every moral rule would have this flaw. It is customary in philosophical writing to ignore this complication when formulating principles—the rule against causing pain may be expressed simply by saying that it is wrong to cause pain—and then to bring the complication in later by adding that such principles are only prima facie or ceteris paribus. However, it will be useful to formulate the principle of equality in such a way as to take this complication into account from the outset, acknowledging the presumptive nature of the principle in its initial statement. Therefore, our principle may be understood as follows: individuals are to be treated in the same way unless there is a relevant difference between them that justifies the difference in treatment.

I believe that this principle expresses, at the deepest level, what is wrong with racism, sexism, and the like. Those practices involve setting individuals apart for different treatment when there are no relevant differences between them that justify it. I have formulated the principle in plain language, and it may be taken to mean exactly what it says. Nevertheless, it contains terms that need to be clarified and explained. The most obvious question is, What is meant by a "relevant" difference? Without an answer to this question, we cannot know how to apply the principle to specific cases. We would have no way of showing that race, for example, is not a relevant difference that justifies treating whites differently from blacks. The development of an adequate theory of relevant differences is, I think, one of the most important unfinished tasks facing social philosophers today. It is the heart of the theory of equality. A complete theory of relevant differences would fill a book—and a big book at that—so I cannot do full justice to the subject here. But I do want to indicate the general shape that I think such a theory should have, by making a few pertinent points.

First, whether a difference between individuals is relevant to justifying a difference in treatment is a matter for rational assessment. Faced with the claim that a difference is relevant, we can ask why it is relevant, and if the discussion is morally serious, we may expect an answer. The answer may then be critically examined by ordinary rational methods and found to be adequate or inadequate. Suppose an employer will hire only whites, not blacks. He is basing his hiring policy on a difference between individuals—a difference in race—but is it a relevant difference that justifies the difference in treatment?

How could it be maintained that racial differences justify differences in treatment? Unfortunately, we do not have to look far to find attempted answers to this question. A great many people have tried to justify racist policies by appealing to a variety of ideas. In the eighteenth and nineteenth centuries, European physiologists argued that the mental capacities of blacks were inferior to those of whites because their brains were different. Today this is known to be false, and less sophisticated racists, without bothering to appeal to science, say simply that blacks are less industrious and less ambitious than whites, that they care less about their circumstances, or that they are deficient in moral virtue. Interestingly, though, as depressing as this litany of prejudice might be, it evidences a realization that mere race cannot be a relevant difference. Some further difference is needed. And once the attempt is made to supply additional differences, the way is open for a demonstration that the alleged differences are not real.

The second thing to notice is that whether a difference between individuals is relevant depends entirely on the kind of treatment that is in question. Think again of the examples mentioned earlier concerning the physicians and the law school admissions committee. A doctor may justify prescribing penicillin for one patient but not for another by pointing out that the first patient has an infection whereas the second does not. However, suppose the law school admissions committee tried to justify admitting one applicant but not another by saying that only one has an infection. Of course that would be silly.

(It would be equally silly for the doctor to say that he gave the one patient penicillin because he had scored well on the law school admissions test.) The moral is that before we can determine whether a difference between individuals is relevant to justifying a difference in treatment, we must know what sort of treatment is in question. A difference between individuals that justifies one sort of difference in treatment will not necessarily justify another sort of difference in treatment.

Once this point is made explicit, it seems obvious. But it has a corollary that is not so obvious: there is almost never any one big difference between members of different groups that is relevant to justifying all types of treatment. This is crucial for understanding the logic of racism. Racism involves treating members of the disadvantaged group differently in lots of ways. But even if there were a difference between whites and blacks that justified different treatment in one respect, it would not necessarily justify differential treatment in other respects. The point may be illustrated by an example in which it seems pretty clear that race *is* a relevant consideration. Suppose you are a public health officer charged with conducting a campaign to combat sickle-cell anemia. You would be justified in concentrating your efforts in the black community, rather than in the white community, because blacks are more vulnerable to this disease. Here there is a good reason for approaching the black community differently, and so there is no violation of the principle of equality. But once it is clear why this difference between blacks and whites justifies this particular difference in treatment, it also becomes clear that this difference would be irrelevant to other possible differences in treatment.

But I have not yet addressed the most important question: How do we determine whether a difference between individuals is relevant to justifying a difference in treatment? Intuitively, we might think this is clear to common sense. But are there any general principles to which we can appeal? Can we specify any general criteria that distinguish relevant from irrelevant considerations?

I suggest that there are two such general principles. The first principle concerns the ability to benefit: individuals may be treated differently if there is a difference in their abilities to benefit from the type of treatment involved. All the examples we have considered so far fall under this principle. Why is the fact that one patient has an infection while another has a broken bone relevant to justifying the decision to give one but not the other penicillin? The explanation is that the person with the infection will benefit from penicillin while the person with the broken bone will not. Similarly, someone who has done well in college and has scored high on the law school admissions test has a better chance of benefiting from law school admission than someone who has a poor record—the assumption is that he or she has a better chance of successfully completing law school and enjoying a career as a lawyer. (If this is not true, then college grades and test scores do not have the relevance that we normally think they have.) And the reason it is permissible to concentrate efforts to combat sickle-cell anemia in the black community is that blacks stand to benefit most from such a campaign. Thus all these examples, which at first seem very different, are actually instances of the same general point.

The second principle concerns desert: individuals may be treated differently if there is a difference in what they deserve. This principle is liable to be more controversial than the first; nevertheless, I believe it expresses an independent and valid criterion. Suppose an employer must choose which of two employees to promote. One has worked hard for the company for several years; she has taken on extra work without complaint, worked overtime without demanding extra pay when the company could not afford it, and so on. The other has not put in nearly so much effort; she has done the least she could get by with. Clearly, the boss has reason to prefer the first employee— she has earned the promotion, and so she deserves it, in a way that the second does not.

Desert is not the same as ability to benefit. Both employees might benefit from the promotion; both could use the extra money and status. Moreover, we might imagine that the second would reform in the new position and work just as diligently. But even allowing this (perhaps unrealistic) assumption, the first employee still has a superior claim on the promotion, based on her work in the past. Desert, whether it is for good or ill, always depends on past conduct.

My hypothesis is that these two principles, taken together, may be used to determine whether any particular difference between individuals is relevant to justifying a difference in treatment. They determine the application of the principle of equality. I do not mean that they define all relevant considerations for the whole sphere of practical decision making. I mean only that they are definitive for one particular (but very important) ideal, the ideal of equal treatment. Other considerations may come into play when the focus is on other principles; but for the principle of equality, these are the important ones.

Clearly there is a lot more that needs to be said on these topics, but I want to pass on now to a somewhat different matter. The principle of equality may be used, as I have indicated, to explain why racist and sexist policies are untenable. But it is also useful in explaining the nature of prejudicial reasoning. In particular, it throws important light on the motivation of racist and sexist stereotypes.

Stereotypes

As we have already observed, racism carries with it an array of unflattering beliefs about its victims: that blacks, for example, are less industrious, less intelligent, and less ambitious than whites; that they care less about their circumstances; that they are deficient in moral virtue. The stereotypes are depressingly familiar. Similar myths have plagued other groups. Jews are avaricious and cunning, not to be trusted. Women are emotional and indecisive. These are also familiar, if depressing, pictures; but they are worth pondering, if not for their truth, for their psychological significance. Why do people believe such things? Why are these myths, so blatantly false, nevertheless so widespread?

Part of the explanation, it is commonly said, is that racism, sexism, and anti-Semitism all involve complex feelings of fear and hostility. Racists and anti-Semites tend to be fearful people, nervous about their own insecure places in society. More generally, it is said, we all tend to identify with others "of our own kind," while suspecting those who are "different." There may be something to this, but it is in a certain sense a superficial observation. There have been too many racists and anti-Semites who were not obviously insecure. Another part of the explanation may be that the myths are sometimes distorted truths. There are historical reasons—connected with the persecution of European Jewry—why many Jews became merchants and bankers; this may help explain why the particular vice attributed to them is avariciousness. In the same vein, it is a fact, at least in some cultures, that women weep more easily than men; and this, regardless of how it is explained, may have contributed to the view of women as overly emotional. But again, while these "truths" may be part of the story, they provide a relatively superficial explanation that does not reach very deep.

The deeper explanation has to do with the principle of equality. I believe that this principle, in addition to being a fundamental normative principle, also has an important descriptive function in moral psychology. It is one of the principles we need when developing a theory about how people think. It is exactly what we need to explain the persistence of the various racist and sexist myths.

Suppose we make two assumptions. The first is that everyone accepts, however unconsciously, the principle of equality. Everyone utilizes it in their thinking. This does not mean that everyone can articulate the principle. People use many principles in their reasoning that they cannot consciously articulate. Anyone who can add or subtract uses principles of arithmetic, but not many can tell you what those principles are—indeed, the discovery of those principles was an important intellectual achievement that required genius. Nevertheless, people do follow the principles in their arithmetical reasoning. Similarly, my assumption is that the principle of equality guides people's moral reasoning, even if they are not aware of it.

The second assumption is that people often benefit from treating members of other groups badly. Slaveholders in the American South benefited from their "peculiar institution" of slavery, just as whites continue to benefit from a system in which blacks supply cheap unskilled labor. Men benefit from a system in which women are paid less and in general from a social arrangement in which they are the bosses. Marx argued that the motivation for such exploitation is always economic; be that as it may, it seems clear that there are advantages to be gained from some groups dominating others—advantages, at least, for those in the dominant group.

If both these assumptions are true—if the principle of equality influences people's reasoning, while they have something to gain by discriminating against members of other groups—a tension is created. Whites, for example, are pulled in two ways: they have reasons of self-interest to discriminate against blacks, but the principle of equality forbids it. How is this tension to be resolved?

This is where the myths come in. The myths resolve the tension by supplying (fictitious) relevant differences between people that make it all right to treat them differently. If blacks were less intelligent, less ambitious, and lazier than whites, it would be perfectly all right not to provide them equal educational opportunities or not to consider them for important jobs. If they were a "childlike race," as it was said in earlier times, then even a benevolent slavery might be justified. The same goes for the myths about women. The view of females as less decisive and less rational than males permits the males to exclude them from positions of power. La Fontaine once remarked that "Those who enjoy power always arrange matters so as to give their tyranny an appearance of justice."[3] Here, the myths create the appearance of justice by supplying the relevant differences demanded by the principle of equality. Thus, the principle of equality not only explains the wrongness of racism, but as a principle of moral psychology, it enables us to explain something of the structure of racist reasoning and the motivation of its main features. In a strange way, the stereotypes persist because the members of the dominant groups are trying, as they should, to maintain a rough consistency between their beliefs and their practice.

Unconscious Prejudice

"Good sense," said Descartes, "is of all things in the world the most equally distributed, for everybody thinks himself so abundantly provided with it, that even those most difficult to please in all other matters do not commonly desire more of it than they already possess."[4] Much the same might be said about impartiality: everyone believes himself or herself to be objective and free of bias. We recognize that other people may be prejudiced, of course, but we imagine that we ourselves see things as they really are.

This is, of course, a mistake. We feel that we are un-prejudiced only because we are unaware of our biases and how they work. This is true not only of bigots but of liberal-minded people as well. It is a mistake for any of us to think that we are immune from tendencies that are well-nigh universal among human beings. Even when we are striving hardest to be objective, prejudices of all sorts can creep into our judgments without our noticing them.

To illustrate this, we may consider a type of example that does not often occur to people. We are familiar enough with prejudice against people on account of their race or gender. But that is not the only way in which we discriminate. There is an impressive body of evidence that we are also prejudiced against people because of their height. I do not mean simply that we are prejudiced against abnormally short or tall people—dwarves or giants. That sort of prejudice is familiar enough. The less widely recognized form of prejudice is against shorter people whose height falls within the normal range. Let me briefly mention some of the investigations that have been conducted into this matter.[5]

In one study, 140 job-placement officers were asked to choose between two applicants with exactly the same qualifications, but one was described, parenthetically, as being 6'1" while the other candidate was said to be 5'5". One hundred and two of the recruiters judged the taller candidate to be better qualified, while only one preferred the shorter candidate. The rest of them—a mere 27 percent—recognized that the two were equally well qualified.

Other studies have shown that a person's earning potential is affected more by height than by educational performance. One study compared the starting salaries of male librarians between 6'1" and 6'3" with the starting salaries of male librarians less than 6'0"; then the same comparison was made between those who had been in the top half of their classes academically and those who had been in the bottom half. The average difference in starting salary between the taller and shorter graduates was found to be more than three times greater than the difference between the salaries of the more and less academically gifted.

Another study using a sample of over 5,000 men found that after twenty-five years of pursuing their varied careers, those who were 5'6" or 5'7" were earning on average $2,500 per year less than those who were 6'0" or 6'1". The moral seems to be: if you could choose between being tall and being smart, from a crass economic standpoint, it is better to be tall.

The same sort of prejudice influences the way we vote. Of all U.S. presidents, only two—James Madison and Benjamin Harrison—were shorter than the average height for American males at the time of their election. And since 1904, the taller candidate has emerged victorious in 80 percent of presidential elections. Another moral might be drawn: if you are trying to predict the outcome of such an election, forget the other factors, and put your money on the taller man.

These facts are quite remarkable. They suggest a number of points that should be of great interest to anyone who is thinking about the philosophical problem of equality, especially as it relates to the formulation and assessment of actual policies. Here I will mention just two such points. First, prejudice can have its influence quite unconsciously. No one—or so nearly no one that it makes no difference—realizes that they think less well of shorter people whose height is well within the normal range. Yet the available evidence shows that this prejudice exists and that it is widespread. The people who are affected by it are simply unaware of it. Second, this evidence suggests that people are very good at rationalizing the judgments they make, even when the real explanation for their judgments is the operation of prejudice. The people whose actions were studied in these investigations—those who hired, promoted, and gave pay raises to the taller candidates—were, no doubt, in most instances reasonable people who could "explain" each decision by reference to the lucky employee's objective qualifications. The behavior that is induced by prejudice includes, importantly, the verbal behavior that "justifies" the prejudiced judgments.

These points, taken together, have a discouraging implication. They suggest that it is difficult even for people of good will to prevent such prejudice from influencing their deliberations. If I am prejudiced in ways that I do not fully realize and skilled at coming up with reasons to "justify" the decisions that this prejudice leads me to make, then my good intention to "think objectively"—no matter how sincerely I want to do this—may be depressingly ineffective.

Why Quotas Are Sometimes Justified

Suppose you are the president of a manufacturing company, and in the course of your business, you need, each year, a supply of widgets. Widgets vary greatly in quality, and from among the hundreds available each year, you need to get the best ten you can find. You are not able to devote your own time to this task, but luckily you have an assistant who is one of the most astute widget-evaluators in the land. "Examine all the available widgets," you tell him, "and bring me the ten best."

In the fullness of time, your assistant brings you ten good widgets, and all seems well. But then you notice that all ten were made at the Buffalo Widget Works. This is odd because you know that the Albany Widget Works makes an equally good product; moreover, you know that the pool from which your assistant made his selection contained equal numbers of Albany widgets and Buffalo widgets. So why should the ten best all come from Buffalo? You would expect that, on average, five would come from Buffalo and five from Albany. But perhaps this was just a statistical fluke, and it will all average out over time.

The next year, however, much the same thing happens again. You need ten widgets, you assign your assistant to identify the best, and he brings you nine made in Buffalo and only one made in Albany. "Why?" you ask, and in response he assures you that, even though the Albany company does make excellent widgets, most of the best ones available this year happened to be from Buffalo. To prove the point, he gives you quite an intelligent and persuasive analysis of the merits of the widgets in this year's pool. You are so impressed that you name him Vice President of Widget Procurement.

But in subsequent years the story is repeated again and again, with only slight variations. Each year you are told that almost all the best available widgets are from Buffalo. You begin to feel sure that something peculiar is going on. Briefly, you wonder whether your VPWP is accepting bribes from the Buffalo company; but you reject that hypothesis. He is an honest fellow, and you cannot help but believe that he is using his best judgment each time he selects widgets for you. Then you consider whether, in fact, the Buffalo widgets are simply better than the Albany widgets. But you reject this possibility also; other experts all agree that the Albany products are equally good.

Finally, you make a discovery that explains everything. It turns out that your vice president was raised in Buffalo, where there is a strong sense of civic pride and an even stronger sense of rivalry with nearby Albany. Children in Buffalo, it seems, have it drilled into them that everything about Buffalo is better than anything about Albany. Moreover, before coming to work for you, your VPWP worked for the Buffalo Chamber of Commerce and was in charge of promoting Buffalo products. Obviously, then, he is prejudiced, and that explains why he almost always judges Buffalo widgets to be superior.

What are you to do? You could forget about it; after all, the widgets you are getting from Buffalo are pretty good. But you do not want to do that; it is important to you to have the very best widgets you can get. So you talk to your VPWP and stress the importance of getting the best widgets regardless of whether they are made in Buffalo or Albany. He is a bit offended by this, however, because he is a good man and he believes himself to be impartial. He assures you that he is selecting the best widgets available, and if they happen to be from Buffalo, he cannot help it. As time passes, nothing changes: he continues to select mostly Buffalo widgets.

Now what? You are certain that he is prejudiced in favor of Buffalo widgets, but because the prejudice is entirely unconscious, your VPWP seems unable to overcome it or even to recognize it. You could get a new VPWP. But you do not want to do that, because this man is excellent except for this one problem. Then an obvious solution occurs to you. You could simply change your instructions to him. Instead of saying, each year, "Bring me the ten best widgets," you could say, "Bring me the five best Buffalo widgets and the five best Albany widgets." He might not like that—he might take it as an insult to his ability to judge widgets impartially—but if it is true that Albany widgets are equally as good as Buffalo widgets, this would result in your getting a better overall quality of widget, on average, year in and year out.[6]

The VPWP might, however, offer an interesting objection. He might point out that, in carrying out your new instructions, he would sometimes have to include an Albany widget that is inferior to a Buffalo widget that was also available. You will have to admit that this is so. But your problem is a practical one. You can trust the VPWP to judge which are the best Albany widgets, and you can trust him to judge which are the best Buffalo widgets. But you cannot trust him to compare objectively the relative merits of a widget from one city with those of a widget from the other city. In these circumstances, the fact remains that your new instructions give you a better chance of ending up with the best overall supply. Or to put it another way, you want the best qualified widgets to get the job done, and the quota system you have established will see to that more effectively than the alternative method of simply allowing you VPWP to exercise his judgment.

Because this example involves the selection of widgets,

not the hiring of people, it is not apt to stir up much passion. But quotas that govern hiring practices do generate a great deal of passion. Of all the kinds of policies that have been devised to combat discrimination, quotas are the least often defended. Almost no one seems willing to say a good word about them. Yet the widget example shows that, under certain circumstances, quotas can be defensible. Quotas in hiring can be justified by the same argument that justifies quotas in widget selection.

Suppose we imagine that you are not the president of a company but the dean of a college, and you are concerned that only the best-qualified scholars are hired for your faculty. You notice, however, that your philosophy department never hires any women. So you investigate. You discover that there are, indeed, lots of female philosophers looking for jobs each year. And you have no reason to think that these women are, on average, any less capable than their male colleagues. So you talk to the (male) chairperson of the philosophy department and urge him to be careful to give full and fair consideration to the female applicants. Being a good liberal fellow, he finds this an agreeable instruction—although he may be a little offended by the suggestion that he is not already doing so. But the talk has little apparent effect. Whenever candidates are being considered, he continues to report, sincerely enough, that in the particular group under review, a male has emerged as the best qualified. "And so," he says with some regret, "if we want to hire the best qualified applicant, we have to hire the male."

After further efforts have been made along these lines, without result, you might eventually conclude that there is an unconscious prejudice at work that cannot be countered by any measure short of issuing a new instruction: you might tell the philosophy department that it must hire some women, in numbers at least in proportion to the number of women in the applicant pool. The reply, of course, will be that this policy could result in hiring a less-qualified woman over a better-qualified man. But the answer is the same as in the example about the widgets. You are not trying to give women a special break, just as you were not trying to give Albany widgets a special break. Nor are you trying to redress the injustices that women have suffered in the past. Nor are you trying to provide "role models" for other women. You may be pleased if your policy has these effects, but the purpose of your policy is not to achieve them. Your only purpose is to get the best-qualified scholars for your faculty, regardless of their gender. Because of unconscious prejudice, the usual system of simply allowing your experts— the philosophy department—to exercise their judgment is an imperfect system for accomplishing that purpose. Allowing them to exercise their judgment within the limits of a quota system, on the other hand, might be a more effective system because it reduces the effect of unconscious prejudice.

Of course, this argument does not purport to show that any system of quotas, applied in any circumstances, is fair. The argument is only a defense of quotas used in a certain way in certain circumstances. But the type of circumstances I have described is not uncommon. Actual quota systems, of the sort that have been established and tested in the courts in recent years, often have just this character: they are instituted to counter the prejudice, conscious or otherwise, that corrupts judgments of merit. Let me cite a real case that illustrates this.

In 1972, there were no blacks in the Alabama State Police. In the thirty-seven year history of the force, there never had been any. The NAACP brought suit to end this vestige of segregation, and federal district court judge Frank Johnson condemned what he termed a "blatant and continuous pattern and practice of discrimination." Judge Johnson did not, however, simply order the Alabama authorities to stop discriminating and to start making their decisions impartially. He knew that such an order would be treated with amused contempt: the authorities would have been only too happy to continue as before, "impartially" finding that no blacks were qualified. So to prevent this and to insure that the Alabamians could not avoid hiring qualified blacks, Johnson ordered that the state must hire and promote one qualified black for every white trooper hired or promoted, until 25 percent of the force was black.

Judge Johnson's order was appealed to the Eleventh Circuit Court, where it was upheld. Time went by while the state was supposed to be carrying out the instruction. In 1984, twelve years later, the district court reviewed the situation to see what progress had been made. Forced by the court to do so, some blacks had been hired but virtually none had been promoted. The court found that among the six majors on the force, none were black. Of the twenty-five captains, none were black. Of the thirty-five lieutenants, none were black. Of the sixty-five sergeants, none were black. Of the sixty-six corporals, however, there were four blacks. The court declared, "This is intolerable and must not continue."[7]

The State of Alabama's last hope was the Supreme Court, which heard the case and rendered its decision in 1987. By a 5 to 4 vote, the Supreme Court upheld Judge Johnson's orders, and the *Birmingham News* ran a front-page story describing the "bitter feelings" of the white troopers, who viewed the ruling as a "setback." A spokesperson for Alabama's Department of Public Safety assured the newspaper, "The department will comply with this ruling." It was clear enough from the official statements, however, that "complying with the ruling" would force the department to take steps—actually promoting blacks—that it would never take voluntarily.[8]

The quota policy mandated by Judge Johnson continues to cause controversy. Nevertheless, this sort of quota is justified as a way of countering the effects of prejudice. I conclude, in the time-honored way, by indicating replies to the various objections that are sure to be made.

> Objection: People ought to be hired or promoted on the basis of their qualifications, not on the basis of their race or gender. To give preference to a black merely because he is black or to a woman merely because she is female is no more defensible than to prefer a white man because he is white or male.
>
> Reply: The whole point of my argument is that quotas may be justified as part of a plan to make sure that people are hired or promoted on the basis of their qualifications. The sort of policy that I have discussed does not involve hiring

or promoting on the basis of race or gender, but only on the basis of qualification. Quota policies are being defended, in some circumstances, only because they are the most effective policies for achieving that goal.

Objection: The white male who is passed over is not responsible for the injustices that were done to blacks in the past; therefore, it is unfair to make him pay the price for it.

Reply: Again, this misses the point entirely. The argument does not envision the use of quotas as a response to past discrimination, but as a way of preventing, or at least minimizing, present discrimination. Sometimes people who defend the use of quotas, or other such policies, defend them as only temporary measures to be used, reluctantly, until racism and sexism have been eliminated. It is true, of course, that if racist or sexist prejudice were eliminated, then there would be no need for race- or gender-based quotas. But unfortunately there is little reason to expect such a vast change in human attitudes any time soon.

Objection: The argument given does not apply to decisions made solely on the basis of objective criteria—test scores, college grades, and the like. We can easily enough imagine procedures that, by using only such objective criteria, leave no room for the operation of prejudice. So the best qualified will win out, and quotas are unnecessary.

Reply: There is a certain amount of truth in this. As I said, this argument is not intended as a defense of the use of quotas in every conceivable circumstance. But consider the range of cases that must be dealt with in the real world. Is there any hiring procedure that a rational person would adopt that would not disclose that an applicant for a teaching job was male or female? Should we be willing to hire teachers without an interview? Is there any imaginable multiple-choice test that we would be willing to use as the sole criterion for promotion in a police department? Should we be willing to eliminate the use of the assessments of those who have observed an officer's performance?

Moreover, it should also be remembered that so-called "objective" criteria often involve the use of tainted evidence. Suppose, in order to be perfectly impartial, I resolve to make a hiring decision using only objective criteria, such as college grades. In this way I prevent any prejudices that I might have from influencing my judgment. So far so good. But the grades themselves were handed out by teachers whose prejudices could have come into play during the grading process. I succeed only in substituting their prejudices for mine.

Objection: Under a policy of quotas, wouldn't there be some instances of injustice (that is, instances in which a less well qualified individual is preferred to a better-qualified individual) that otherwise would not occur? And isn't this inherently unfair?

Reply: Of course this will inevitably happen. But the question is whether there would be fewer injustices under this policy than under the alternative of "hiring strictly according to qualifications," which means, in practice, hiring according to judgments of qualifications made by biased judges. Some philosophers have urged that it is not acceptable to treat someone unjustly for the purpose of preventing other injustices—but that point, even if it is correct, does not apply here. The choice here is between two policies, neither of which is perfect and each of which would inevitably involve some injustices. The relevant question is, which policy would involve less injustice?

The argument I have presented turns on taking into account an important fact about human beings, unconscious prejudice. Frequently philosophers think about justice in isolation from such facts. The question about quotas is often put this way: assuming that X is a highly qualified white man and Y is a somewhat less qualified black or woman, would it be right to hire Y ahead of X? Then, after arguing that this would not be right, the writer concludes that quotas are, in principle, unjust. But this is a thoughtless conclusion that does little justice to the complexity of the real world. In the real world people do not come prelabeled as better or worse qualified; someone has to make that judgment, and that is where prejudice is most likely to enter the picture. Yet the philosophers' hypothetical question arises only after such judgments have already been made. Philosophers should not lend their weight and support (little though it may be), or their opposition, to real-world policies, when their arguments apply only to hypothetical situations that differ from the real world in important ways.

Notes

1. Claude Adrien Helvétius, *A Treatise on Man*, 2 vols. (Paris: Chez la Société Typographique, 1773), introduction.

2. Leon Trotsky, *Literature and Revolution*, trans. Rose Strunsky (Ann Arbor, Mich.: University of Michigan Press, 1960), p. 256.

3. Jean La Fontaine, *The Fables of La Fontaine*, trans. Marianne Moore (New York: Viking Press, 1952), p. 162.

4. Elizabeth S. Haldane and G. R. T. Ross, *The Philosophical Works of Descartes*, 2 vols. (New York: Dover Books, 1955), vol. 1, p. 81.

5. The following information concerning prejudice based on a person's height is from John S. Gillis, *Too Tall, Too Small* (Champaign, Ill.: Institute for Personality and Ability Testing, 1982).

6. Although the proof of this may be obvious, perhaps it is worthwhile to spell it out. If we assume that Albany widgets are, on average, as good as Buffalo widgets, we are assuming something like this: the best Albany widget is likely to be as good as the best Buffalo widget. The second-best Albany widget, although it is not as good as the best Albany widget, is likely to be as good as the second-best Buffalo widget, although that Buffalo widget is not as good as the best Buffalo widget. The third-best Albany widget is likely to be as good as the third-best Buffalo widget. And so on. Therefore, a group that includes Buffalo widgets 1–8 and Albany widgets 1–2 will not be as good as the group that includes the five best widgets from each source. It is tempting to object that our assumption—that Albany widgets are on average as good as Buffalo widgets—does not guarantee this sort of one-to-one correlation. That is true, but if we are assuming that quality is randomly distributed in the two groups—rather than, say, that one group dominates in the upper half of the pool—then one-to-one correlation is a reasonable model of the distribution.

7. James J. Kilpatrick, "Reverse Discrimination Is Still Discrimination," *Birmingham News*, November 5, 1986, p. 9A.

8. Stan Bailey, "Troopers Hope Bitter Feeling Goes," *Birmingham News*, February 26, 1987, p. 1.

4

How to Make People Moral

James P. Sterba

The Implausibility of Moral Relativism

Many people think that morality is a matter of opinion and that what is right for you may be wrong for me even if we are similarly situated. Such people are moral relativists, and they take their view to be amply supported by the diverse moral views held in different societies as well as by the level of moral disagreement that exists within any given society, such as our own. In our own society, there is presently radical disagreement over abortion, welfare, capital punishment, and arms control, to name but a few issues. Yet these disagreements seem to pale when our society is compared with other societies that presently condone apartheid, infanticide, polygamy, euthanasia, and even cannibalism.

Nevertheless, in order for moral relativists to draw support for their view from this moral diversity, they must be able to show that the same act could be both right and wrong—right for one society, group, or individual, and wrong for some other society, group, or individual. Frequently, however, the act that is condemned by one society, group, or individual is not the same act that is sanctioned by another society, group, or individual. For example, the voluntary euthanasia that is sanctioned by Eskimos as a transition to what they take to be a happier existence for their aged members is significantly different from the euthanasia that we forbid our doctors from practicing.[1] Likewise, when the Nuer gently lay their deformed infants in the river because they believe that such infants are baby hippos accidentally born to humans, their action is significantly different from the infanticide we condemn.[2]

Moreover, even when the same act is being compared, there is a need to distinguish between what people think is right for them to do and what is right for them to do. For people may think that an act is right for them to do only because they are insufficiently informed with respect to the relevant facts or because they reasoned incorrectly with respect to those facts. With regard to either of these deficiencies, people may or may not be culpable. If they are culpable, they can be blamed for the discrepancy between what they think is right and what is right. If they are not culpable, they cannot be so blamed, because correcting that deficiency was beyond their control.

Furthermore, for an act to be right for someone to do, it must have been possible for that individual under ideal conditions to come to perceive that act as right. Acts that are inaccessible to people's best judgment even under ideal conditions (like avoiding carcinogens in the Middle Ages) are not acts that could be morally right for them to do. Accordingly, when we evaluate people's moral judgments in the context in which they formed them, it will sometimes be the case that they could not have arrived at the judgments we think are morally right, or even if they could have done so under ideal conditions, under existing conditions they may not be culpable for not doing so. In either case, their judgments would not relevantly conflict with our own, even if what they think is right is not what we think is right. Consequently, in order for moral relativism to draw support from the existing moral diversity, we must be able to find at least two acts that are relevantly similar: one that could be judged right by someone under ideal conditions, the other that could be judged wrong by someone else under ideal conditions.

But even this is not enough. Moral relativism must also tell us what morality is supposed to be relative to. Is it to be relative to the common beliefs of a society, to those of a smaller group, or to those of just any individual, or could it be relative to any of these? If it could be relative to any of these, any act (for example, killing by contract), could be wrong from the point of view of some particular society, right from the point of view of some subgroup of that society (for example, the Mafia), and wrong again from the point of view of some particular member of that society or subgroup. But if this is the case, individuals would not have any reasonable grounds for deciding what they ought to do, all things considered.

Yet even supposing that some particular reference group could be shown to be preferable (for example, the reference group of an individual's own society), problems remain. First, in deciding what to do, should we simply ask what the members of our appropriate reference group think ought to be done? But if everyone in our reference group did the same, we would all be waiting for everyone else to decide, and so no one would decide what ought to be done. Or we might construe moral relativism to be a second-order theory that requires that the members of our appropriate reference group first decide on some other grounds what is right and then take a vote. If a majority or a consensus emerges from such a vote, then that is what is right, all things considered. So interpreted, "moral relativism" would have some merit as a theory of collective decision making, but it clearly would require some yet-to-be-determined nonrelativist grounds for first-order moral judgments, and so it would not essentially be a relativist theory at all.

Second, the very claim that morality should be specified relativistically is not itself a relativistic claim. Rather it claims to be a truth for all times and places. But how could this be possible? Shouldn't the truth of relativism itself be assertible as a relativistic claim? Now one might maintain that while moral judgments are relativistic, the thesis of moral relativism is not itself a moral claim and, hence, need not be relativistic. But if truth is not relativistic, why should the good be relativistic?

In sum, moral relativism as an account of moral judgments faces a number of difficulties. First, it is difficult for moral relativists to show that amid the existing moral diversity there are actually relevantly similar acts that could be judged right by some and wrong by others under ideal conditions. Second, it is difficult for moral relativists to specify the appropriate reference group from which morality is to be determined. Third, even assuming the appropriate reference group could be determined, it is difficult for moral relativists to explain why their theory is not committed to some nonrelativist account of at least first-order moral judgments. Lastly, it is difficult for moral relativists to explain why they are committed to a nonrelativist account of truth.

Yet while these difficulties obviously render moral relativism an implausible theory, they do not completely defeat it in the absence of a better account of moral judgments. In order to provide such an account, I now wish to show how it is possible to make people moral by the force of argument. My argument has two steps. First, I will show how morality is a requirement of rationality, and second, I will begin to show how morality imposes the same basic practical requirements on everyone.

Now once you see the implausibility of moral relativism, the main challenge to morality comes from rational egoism. This is because rational egoism is a nonrelativist alternative to morality. Accordingly, in offering my justification of morality, I will be attempting as far as possible to find premises that do not beg the questions against rational egoism.

Let us begin by imagining that we are as members of a society deliberating over what sort of principles governing action we should accept. Let us assume that each of us is capable of entertaining and acting upon both self-interested and moral reasons and that the question we are seeking to answer is what sort of principles governing action it would be rational for us to accept.[3] This question is not about what sort of principles we should publicly affirm, since people will sometimes publicly affirm principles that are quite different from those they are prepared to act upon, but rather it is about what principles it would be rational for us to accept at the deepest level—in our heart of hearts.

Of course, there are people who are incapable of acting upon moral reasons. For such people, there is no question about their being required to act morally or altruistically. But the interesting philosophical question is not about such people but about people, like ourselves, who are capable of acting self-interestedly or morally and are seeking a rational justification for following one course of action over the others.

Obviously, from a self-interested perspective, the only principles we should accept are those that can be derived from the following general principle of egoism: each person ought to do what best serves his or her overall self-interest. But we can no more defend egoism by simply denying the relevance of moral reasons to rational choice than we can, by simply denying the relevance of self-interested reasons to rational choice, defend the view of pure altruism that the principles we should accept are those that can be derived from the following general principle of altruism: each person ought to do what best serves the overall interest of others. Consequently, in order not to beg the question against either egoism or altruism, we seem to have no other alternative but to grant the prima facie relevance of both self-interested and moral reasons to rational choice and then to try to determine which reasons we would be rationally required to act upon, all things considered.

In this regard, there are two kinds of cases that must be considered. First, there are cases in which there is a conflict between the relevant self-interested and moral reasons.[4] Second, there are cases in which there is no such conflict.

Now it seems obvious that where there is no conflict and both reasons are conclusive reasons of their kind, both reasons should be acted upon. In such contexts, we should do what is favored both by morality and by self-interest. Consider the following example. Suppose you accepted a job marketing a baby formula in underdeveloped countries, where the formula was improperly used, leading to increased infant mortality.[5] Imagine that you could just as well have accepted an equally attractive and rewarding job marketing a similar formula in developed countries, where the misuse does not occur, so that a rational weighing of the relevant self-interested reasons alone would not have favored your acceptance of one of these jobs over the other.[6] At the same time, there were obviously moral reasons that condemned your acceptance of the first job—reasons that you presumably are or were able to acquire. Moreover, by assumption in this case, the moral reasons do not clash with the relevant self-interested reasons; they simply made a recommendation while the relevant self-interested reasons were silent. Consequently, a rational weighing of all the relevant reasons in this case could not but favor acting in accord with the relevant moral reasons.[7]

Yet it might be objected that in cases of this sort there would frequently be other reasons significantly opposed to these moral reasons—other reasons that you are or were able to acquire. Such reasons would be either *malevolent* reasons seeking to bring about the suffering and death of other human beings, *benevolent* reasons concerned to promote nonhuman welfare even at the expense of human welfare, or *aesthetic* reasons concerned to produce valuable results irrespective of the effects on human or nonhuman welfare. But assuming that such malevolent reasons are ultimately rooted in some conception of what is good for oneself or others,[8] these reasons would have already been taken into account and by assumption outweighed by the other relevant reasons in this case. And although neither benevolent reasons (concerned to promote nonhuman welfare) nor aesthetic reasons would have been taken into account, such reasons are not directly relevant to justifying morality to the rational egoist.[9] Consequently, even with the presence of these three kinds of reasons, your acceptance of the first job can still be seen to be contrary to the relevant reasons in this case.

Needless to say, defenders of rational egoism cannot but be disconcerted with this result, since it shows that actions that accord with rational egoism are contrary to reason, at least when there are two equally good ways of pursuing one's self-interest, only one of which does not conflict with the basic requirements of morality. Notice also that in cases where there are two equally good ways of fulfilling the basic requirements of morality, only one of which does not conflict with what is in a person's overall self-interest, it is not at all disconcerting for defenders of morality to admit that we are rationally required to choose the way that does not conflict with what is in our overall self-interest. Nevertheless, exposing this defect in rational egoism for cases where moral reasons and self-interested reasons do not conflict would be but a small victory for defenders of morality if it were not also possible to show that in cases where such reasons do conflict, moral reasons would have priority over self-interested reasons.

Now when we rationally assess the relevant reasons in such conflict cases, it is best to cast the conflict not as a conflict between self-interested reasons and moral reasons but instead as a conflict between self-interested reasons and altruistic reasons.[10] Viewed in this way, three solutions are possible. First, we could say that self-interested reasons always have priority over conflicting altruistic reasons. Second, we could say, just the opposite, that altruistic reasons always have priority over conflicting self-interested reasons. Third, we could say that some kind of compromise is rationally required. In this compromise, sometimes self-interested reasons would have priority over altruistic reasons, and sometimes altruistic reasons would have priority over self-interested reasons.

Once the conflict is described in this manner, the third solution can be seen to be the one that is rationally required. This is because the first and second solutions give exclusive priority to one class of relevant reasons over the other, and only a completely question-begging justification can be given for such an exclusive priority. Only by employing the third solution, and sometimes giving priority to self-interested reasons and sometimes giving priority to altruistic reasons, can we avoid a completely question-begging resolution.

Consider the following example. Suppose you are in the waste disposal business and you decided to dispose of toxic wastes in a manner that was cost-efficient for you but predictably causes significant harm to future generations. Imagine that there were alternative methods available for disposing of the waste that were only slightly less cost-efficient and that did not cause any significant harm to future generations.[11] In this case, you are to weigh your self-interested reasons favoring the most cost-efficient disposal of the toxic wastes against the relevant altruistic reasons favoring the avoidance of significant harm to future generations. If we suppose that the projected loss of benefit to yourself was ever so slight and the projected harm to future generations was ever so great, then a nonarbitrary compromise between the relevant self-interested and altruistic reasons would have to favor the altruistic reasons in this case. Hence, as judged by a non-question-begging standard of rationality, your method of waste disposal was contrary to the relevant reasons.

Notice also that this standard of rationality would not support just any compromise between the relevant self-interested and altruistic reasons. The compromise must be a nonarbitrary one, for otherwise it would beg the questions with respect to the opposing egoistic and altruistic views. Such a compromise would have to respect the rankings of self-interested and altruistic reasons imposed by the egoistic and altruistic views, respectively. Since for each individual there is a separate ranking of that individual's relevant self-interested and altruistic reasons, we can represent these rankings from the most important reasons to the least important reasons as follows:

Individual A		Individual B	
Self-Interested Reasons	Altruistic Reasons	Self-Interested Reasons	Altruistic Reasons
1	1	1	1
2	2	2	2
3	3	3	3
—	—	—	—
—	—	—	—
—	—	—	—
N	N	N	N

Accordingly, any nonarbitrary compromise among such reasons in seeking not to beg the questions against the egoism or altruism will have to give priority to those reasons that rank highest in each category. Failure to give priority to the highest-ranking altruistic or self-interested reasons would, other things being equal, be contrary to reason.

Of course, there will be cases in which the only way to avoid being required to do what is contrary to your highest-ranking reasons is by requiring someone else to do what is contrary to his or her highest-ranking reasons. Such cases are sometimes called "lifeboat cases." But while such cases are surely difficult to resolve (maybe only a chance mechanism can offer a reasonable resolution), they surely do not reflect the typical conflict between the relevant self-interested and altruistic reasons that we are, or were, able to acquire. Typically one or the other of the conflicting reasons will rank higher on its respective scale, thus permitting a clear resolution.

Now it is important to see how morality can be viewed as just such a nonarbitrary compromise between self-interested and altruistic reasons. First, a certain amount of self-regard is morally required or at least morally acceptable. Where this is the case, high-ranking self-interested reasons have priority over low-ranking altruistic reasons. Second, morality obviously places limits on the extent to which people should pursue their own self-interest. Where this is the case, high-ranking altruistic reasons have priority over low-ranking self-interested reasons. In this way, morality can be seen to be a nonarbitrary compromise between self-interested and altruistic reasons, and the "moral reasons" that constitute that compromise can be seen as having an absolute priority over the self-interested or altruistic reasons that conflict with them.

Now it might be objected that although the egoistic and the altruistic views are admittedly question-begging, the compromise view is equally so and, hence, is in no way preferable to the other views. In response, I deny that the compromise view is equally question-begging when compared with the egoistic and altruistic views, but I concede that the view is to a lesser degree question-begging nonetheless. For a completely non-question-begging view starts with assumptions that are acceptable to all sides of a dispute. However, the assumption of the compromise view that the highest-ranking altruistic reasons have priority over conflicting lower-ranking self-interested reasons is not acceptable from an egoistic perspective. Nor is the compromise view's assumption that the highest-ranking self-interested reasons have priority over conflicting lower-ranking altruistic reasons acceptable from an altruistic perspective. So one part of what the compromise view assumes about the priority of reasons is not acceptable from an egoistic perspective and another part is not acceptable from an altruistic perspective; hence, to that extent the compromise view does beg the question against each view. Nevertheless, since the whole of what egoism assumes about the priority of reasons is unacceptable from an altruistic perspective and the whole of what altruism assumes about the priority of reasons is unacceptable from an egoistic perspective, each of these views begs the question against the other to a far greater extent than the compromise view does against each of them. Consequently, on the grounds of being the least question-begging, the compromise view is the only nonarbitrary resolution of the conflict between egoism and altruism.

Notice, too, that this defense of morality succeeds not only against the view that egoism is rationally preferable to morality but also against the view that egoism is only rationally on a par with morality. The "weaker view" does not claim that we all ought to be egoists. Rather it claims that there is just as good reason for us to be egoists as there is for us to be pure altruists or anything in between. Kai Nielson summarizes this view: "We have not been able to show that reason requires the moral point of view or that all really rational persons not be individual egoists. Reason doesn't decide here."[12] Yet since the above defense of morality shows morality to be the only nonarbitrary resolution of the conflict between self-interested and altruistic reasons, it is not the case that there is just as good reason for us to endorse morality as there is for us to endorse rational egoism or pure altruism. Thus, the above defense of morality succeeds against the weaker as well as the stronger interpretation of rational egoism.

It might be objected that this defense of morality could be undercut if in the debate over egoism, altruism, and morality, we simply give up any attempt to provide a non-question-begging defense for any one of these views. But we cannot rationally do this. For we are engaged in this debate as people who could act self-interestedly, could act altruistically, could act morally; and we are trying to discover which of these ways of acting is rationally justified. To resolve this question rationally, we have to be committed to deliberating in a non-question-begging manner as far as possible. So as far as I can tell, there is no escaping the conclusion that morality can be given a non-question-begging defense over egoism and altruism.[13]

Unfortunately, this approach to defending morality has been generally neglected by previous moral theorists. The reason for this is that such theorists have tended to cast the basic conflict with rational egoism as a conflict between morality and self-interest. For example, according to Kurt Baier, "the very *raison d'etre* of a morality is to yield reasons which overrule the reasons of self-interest in those cases when everyone's following self-interest would be harmful to everyone."[14] Viewed in this light, it did not seem possible for the defender of morality to be supporting a compromise view, for how could such a defender say that when morality and self-interest conflict, morality should sometimes be sacrificed for the sake of self-interest? But while previous theorists understood correctly that moral reasons could not be compromised in favor of self-interested reasons, they failed to recognize that this is because moral reasons are already the result of a nonarbitrary compromise between self-interested and altruistic reasons. Thus, unable to see how morality could be represented as a compromise solution, previous theorists have generally failed to recognize this approach to defending morality.

A Practical Reconciliation of Opposing Moral Ideals

Of course, exactly how this compromise is to be worked out is a matter of considerable debate. Libertarians with their

ideal of the common good, feminists with their ideal of androgyny, and socialists with their ideal of equality all seem to favor
different practical requirements. My own view, however, is that
when these different ideals are correctly interpreted, they all
lead to the same practical requirements, which just happen to
be those usually associated with a welfare liberal ideal, namely,
a right to welfare and a right to equal opportunity. [15]

But are these rights really required by each of these four
ideals? Certainly no one would deny that these rights are required by a welfare liberal ideal of fairness, assuming that the
ideal is interpreted, as John Rawls has proposed, to involve
hypothetical choice from behind a veil of ignorance that is thick
enough to secure impartiality but thin enough to make unan-
imous agreement possible. This is because even if Rawls's critics are correct in claiming that persons behind such a veil of
ignorance would not seek to maximize the payoffs to the least
advantaged in society, it is certainly the case that persons so
situated would favor rights to equal opportunity and welfare.
Nevertheless, many would surely want to deny that these rights
are also required by one or another of the other three ideals I
mentioned.

Now I do not have the space here to argue that all four of
these ideals require rights to equal opportunity and welfare. To
begin to make my case, however, I will simply argue that the
ideal that initially seems most opposed to such rights, the libertarian ideal of liberty, when correctly interpreted, can be seen
to require the same rights to equal opportunity and welfare that
are required by a welfare liberal ideal.

Now the libertarian ideal of liberty has been defended
in basically two different ways. Some libertarians, following
Herbert Spencer, have (1) taken a right to liberty as basic and
(2) derived all other rights from this right to liberty. Other libertarians, following John Locke, have (1) taken a set of rights,
including typically a right to life and a right to property, as basic
and (2) defined liberty as the absence of constraints in the exercise of these rights. Now both groups of libertarians regard
liberty as the ultimate political ideal, but they do so for different
reasons. For Spencerian libertarians, liberty is the ultimate po-

litical ideal because all other rights are derived from a right to liberty. For Lockean libertarians, liberty is the ultimate political ideal because liberty is just the absence of constraints in the exercise of people's fundamental rights.[16]

Let us begin by considering the view of Spencerian libertarians, who take a right to liberty to be basic and define all other rights in terms of this right to liberty. This view adopts the *want interpretation of liberty*: liberty is being unconstrained by other persons from doing what one wants. Now this interpretation limits the scope of liberty in two ways. First, not all constraints whatever their source count as a restriction of liberty; the constraints must come from other persons. For example, people who are constrained by natural forces from getting to the top of Mount Everest do not lack liberty in this regard. Second, constraints that have their source in other persons but that do not run counter to an individual's wants constrain without restricting that individual's liberty. Thus, people who do not want to hear Beethoven's Fifth Symphony, the fact that others have effectively proscribed its performance does not restrict their liberty, even though it does constrain what they are able to do.

Of course, libertarians may wish to argue that even such constraints can be seen to restrict a person's liberty once we take into account the fact that people normally want, or have a general desire, to be unconstrained by others. But other philosophers have thought that the possibility of such constraints points to a serious defect in this conception of liberty,[17] which can only be remedied by adopting the broader, *ability interpretation of liberty*: liberty is being unconstrained by other persons from doing what one is able to do. Applying this interpretation to the above example, we find that people's liberty to hear Beethoven's Fifth Symphony would be restricted even if they did not want to hear it (and even if, perchance, they did not want to be unconstrained by others), since other people would still be constraining them from doing what they are able to do.

Yet even if we accept all the liberties specified by the ability interpretation, we still need to decide what is to count as a constraint. On the one hand, libertarians would like to limit constraints to positive acts (that is, acts of commission) that prevent people from doing what they are otherwise able to do. On the other hand, welfare liberals and socialists interpret constraints to include, in addition, negative acts (that is, acts of omission) that prevent people from doing what they are otherwise able to do. In fact, this is one way to understand the debate between defenders of "negative liberty" and defenders of "positive liberty." For defenders of negative liberty would seem to interpret constraints to include only positive acts of others that prevent people from doing what they otherwise are able to do, while defenders of positive liberty would seem to interpret constraints to include both positive and negative acts of others that prevent people from doing what they are otherwise able to do.[18]

Now suppose we interpret constraints in the manner favored by libertarians to include only positive acts by others that prevent people from doing what they are otherwise able to do. Interpreting their ideal in this way, libertarians claim to derive a number of more specific requirements—in particular, a right to life; a right to freedom of speech, press, and assembly; and a right to property.

Here it is important to observe that the libertarian's right to life is not a right to receive from others the goods and resources necessary for preserving one's life; it is simply a right not to be killed unjustly. Correspondingly, the libertarian's right to property is not a right to receive from others the goods and resources necessary for one's welfare but rather a right to acquire goods and resources either by initial acquisitions or by voluntary agreements.

Of course, libertarians would allow that it would be nice of the rich to share their surplus resources with the poor. Nevertheless, according to libertarians, such acts of charity should not be coercively required. For this reason, libertarians are opposed to coercively supported welfare programs.

For a similar reason, libertarians are opposed to coercively supported equal opportunity programs. This is because the educational and job opportunities one has under a libertarian ideal of liberty are usually a function of the property one controls, and since unequal property distributions are taken to be justified under a libertarian ideal of liberty, unequal educational and job opportunities are also regarded as justified.

The same results with respect to welfare and equal opportunity obtain for Lockean libertarians, who take a set of rights, typically including a right to life and a right to property, as basic and then adopt the *rights interpretation of liberty:* liberty is being unconstrained by other persons from doing what one has a right to do. According to this view, a right to life is simply a right not to be killed unjustly; it is not a right to receive the goods and resources necessary for preserving one's life. Correspondingly, a right to property is a right to acquire property either by initial acquisition or by voluntary transactions; it is not a right to receive from others whatever goods and resources one needs to maintain oneself. Understanding a right to life and a right to property in this way, libertarians reject both coercively supported welfare and equal opportunity programs as violations of liberty.

Now, in order to see why libertarians are mistaken about what their ideal requires, consider a typical conflict situation between the rich and the poor. In this conflict situation, the rich, of course, have more than enough resources to satisfy their basic needs. By contrast, the poor lack the resources to meet their most basic needs even though they have tried all the means available to them that libertarians regard as legitimate for acquiring such resources. Under circumstances like these, Spencerian libertarians usually maintain that the rich should have the liberty to use their resources to satisfy their luxury needs if they so wish. Spencerian libertarians recognize that this liberty might well be enjoyed at the expense of the satisfaction of the most basic needs of the poor; they just think that liberty always has priority over other moral ideals, and since they assume that the liberty of the poor is not at stake in such conflict situations, it is easy for them to conclude that the rich should not be required to sacrifice their liberty so that the basic needs of the poor may be met.

Of course, Spencerian libertarians would allow that it

would be nice of the rich to share their surplus resources with the poor. Nevertheless, according to Spencerian libertarians, such acts of charity are not required because the liberty of the poor is not thought to be at stake in such conflict situations.

In fact, however, the liberty of the poor is at stake in such conflict situations. What is at stake is the liberty of the poor to take from the surplus possessions of the rich what is necessary to satisfy their basic needs.[19] Needless to say, Spencerian libertarians would want to deny that the poor have this liberty. But how could they justify such a denial? As this liberty of the poor has been specified, it is not a positive right to receive something but a negative right of noninterference. Spencerian libertarians cannot appeal to a right to life or a right to property to rule out such a liberty, because on the Spencerian view liberty is basic and all other rights are derived from a right to liberty. Clearly, what Spencerian libertarians must do is recognize the existence of such a liberty and then claim that it conflicts with other liberties of the rich. But when Spencerian libertarians see that this is the case, they are often genuinely surprised—one might even say rudely awakened—for they had not previously seen the conflict between the rich and poor as a conflict of liberties.[20]

Now when the conflict between the rich and the poor is viewed as a conflict of liberties, either we can say that the rich should have the liberty to use their surplus resources for luxury purposes, or we can say that the poor should have the liberty to take from the rich what they require to meet their basic needs. If we choose one liberty, we must reject the other. What needs to be determined, therefore, is which liberty is morally preferable: the liberty of the rich or the liberty of the poor.

Two Principles

In order to see that the liberty of the poor to take from the surplus resources of others what is required to meet their basic needs is morally preferable to the liberty of the rich to use their surplus resources for luxury purposes, first we need to appeal to one of the most fundamental principles of morality, one that is common to all political perspectives. This is the *"ought" implies "can" principle*: people are not morally required to do what they lack the power to do or what would involve so great a sacrifice that it would be unreasonable to require them to perform such an action.[21] For example, suppose I promised to attend a departmental meeting on Friday, but on Thursday I am involved in a serious car accident that puts me into a coma. Surely it is no longer the case that I ought to attend the meeting, now that I lack the power to do so. Or suppose instead that on Thursday I develop a severe case of pneumonia for which I am hospitalized. Surely I could legitimately claim that I no longer ought to attend the meeting, on the grounds that the risk to my health involved in attending is a sacrifice that it would be unreasonable to require me to bear. In this latter case, the underlying rationale is that I cannot be morally required to sacrifice the satisfaction of my most fundamental interests so that others can satisfy their peripheral interests, unless I have freely chosen to make such a sacrifice.

Now, applying the "ought" implies "can" principle to the case at hand, it seems clear that the poor have it within their power to relinquish willingly such an important liberty as the liberty to take from the rich what they require to meet their basic needs. Nevertheless, it would be unreasonable to require them to make so great a sacrifice. In the extreme case, it would involve requiring the poor to sit back and starve to death. Of course, the poor may have no real alternative to relinquishing this liberty. To do anything else may involve worse consequences for themselves and their loved ones and may invite a painful death. Accordingly, we may expect that the poor would acquiesce, albeit unwillingly, to a political system that denies them the social minimum supported by such a liberty, at the same time that we recognize that such a system imposes an unreasonable sacrifice upon the poor—a sacrifice that we cannot morally blame the poor for trying to evade.[22] Analogously, we might expect that a woman whose life was threatened would submit to a rapist's demands, at the same time that we recognize the utter unreasonableness of those demands.

By contrast, it would not be unreasonable to require the rich to sacrifice the liberty to meet some of their luxury needs so that the poor can have the liberty to meet their basic needs.[23] Naturally, we might expect that the rich, for reasons of self-interest and past contribution, might be disinclined to make such a sacrifice. We might even suppose that the past contribution of the rich provides a good reason for not sacrificing their liberty to use their surplus for luxury purposes. Yet, unlike the poor, the rich could not claim that relinquishing such a liberty involved so great a sacrifice that it would be unreasonable to require them to make it; unlike the poor, the rich could be morally blameworthy for failing to make such a sacrifice.

Notice that in virtue of the "ought" implies "can" principle, this argument establishes that

> 1a. since it would be unreasonable to require the poor to sacrifice the liberty not to be interfered with when taking from the surplus resources of the rich what is necessary to meet their basic needs,
> 1b. it is not the case that the poor are morally required to make such a sacrifice; and
> 2a. since it would not be unreasonable to require the rich to sacrifice the liberty not to be interfered with when using their surplus resources for luxury purposes,
> 2b. it may be the case that the rich are morally required to make such a sacrifice.

What the argument does not establish is that it is the case that the rich are *morally required* to sacrifice (some of) their surplus so that the basic needs of the poor can be met. To establish that conclusion, another widely accepted principle concerning the nature of morality must also be assumed. This is the *conflict resolution principle*: moral resolutions of severe interpersonal conflicts of interests must be reasonable to require everyone affected to accept. This principle accords with the generally accepted view of morality as a system of reasons for resolving interpersonal conflicts of interest. Of course, morality is not limited to such a system of reasons. Most surely it also includes reasons of self-development. All that is being claimed by the principle is that moral resolutions of severe interpersonal conflicts of interest cannot be contrary to reason to require anyone affected to accept. Moreover, when interpersonal conflicts of interest are not severe, moral resolutions must still be reasonable for everyone affected to accept, but they need not be reasonable to *require* that everyone affected accept. This is because not all moral resolutions can be justifiably enforced; only moral resolutions that are reasonable to require that everyone affected accept can be justifiably enforced.

Now, applying the conflict resolution principle to our example of severe conflict between the rich and the poor, there are two possible moral resolutions:

> I. A moral resolution that would require the rich to sacrifice the liberty not to be interfered with when using their surplus resources for luxury purposes so that the poor can have the liberty not to be interfered with when taking from the surplus resources of the rich what is necessary to meet their basic needs
>
> II. A moral resolution that would require the poor to sacrifice the liberty not to be interfered with when taking from the surplus resources of the rich what is necessary to meet their basic needs so that the rich can have the liberty not to be interfered with when using the surplus resources for luxury purposes

These are the only two possible moral resolutions, because in this severe conflict-of-interest situation, if the rich are not required to sacrifice their liberty not to be interfered with when using their surplus resources for luxury purposes, they will be in a position to require effectively the poor to sacrifice their liberty not to be interfered with when taking from the surplus resources of the rich what is necessary to satisfy their basic needs. In such conflict situations, therefore, either the rich or the poor will be required to sacrifice their relevant liberty. If the rich are not (morally) required to sacrifice their relevant liberty, the poor will be coercively required to sacrifice theirs; and if the poor are not (morally) required to sacrifice their relevant liberty, the rich will at least be morally required—and ideally, if necessary, coercively required—to sacrifice theirs.

Our previous discussion of the "ought" implies "can" principle shows that of these two possible moral resolutions, only (I) is reasonable for both the rich and the poor to accept. This is because (1a) rules out (II) but (2a) does not rule out (I). So only (I) satisfies the conflict resolution principle. Consequently, if we assume that however else we specify the requirements of morality, they cannot violate the "ought" implies "can" principle or the conflict resolution principle, it follows that despite what Spencerian libertarians claim, the basic right to liberty endorsed by them, as determined by a weighing of the relevant competing liberties according to these two principles, actually favors the liberty of the poor over the liberty of the rich.

Yet couldn't Spencerian libertarians object to this conclusion, claiming that it would be unreasonable to require the rich to sacrifice the liberty to meet some of their luxury needs so that the poor could have the liberty to meet their basic needs? As has been pointed out, libertarians do not usually see the situation as a conflict of liberties, but suppose they did. How plausible would such an objection be? Not very plausible at all.

For what are Spencerian libertarians going to say about the poor? Isn't it clearly unreasonable to require the poor to sacrifice the liberty to meet their basic needs so that the rich can have the liberty to meet their luxury needs? Isn't it clearly unreasonable to require the poor to sit back and starve to death? If it is, then there is no resolution of this conflict that would be reasonable to require both the rich and the poor to accept. But that would mean that libertarians could not be putting forth a moral resolution, because according to the conflict resolution principle, in cases of severe conflict of interest, a moral resolution resolves conflicts of interest in ways that it would be reasonable to require everyone affected to accept. Therefore, as long as libertarians think of themselves as putting forth a moral resolution for cases of severe conflict of interest, they cannot allow that it would be unreasonable both to require the rich to sacrifice the liberty to meet some of their luxury needs in order to benefit the poor and to require the poor to sacrifice the liberty to meet their basic needs in order to benefit the rich. But I submit that if one of these requirements is to be judged reasonable, then, by any neutral assessment, it must be the requirement that the rich sacrifice the liberty to meet some of their luxury needs so that the poor can have the liberty to meet their basic needs; there is no other plausible resolution if libertarians intend to be putting forth a moral resolution.

But might not Spencerian libertarians hold that putting forth a moral resolution requires nothing more than being willing to universalize one's fundamental commitments? Surely we have no difficulty imagining the rich willing to universalize their commitments to relatively strong property rights. At the same time, we have no difficulty imagining the poor and their advocates being willing to universalize their commitment to relatively weak property rights. However, if a libertarian moral resolution is interpreted in this fashion, it would not be able to provide a basis for resolving conflicts of interest between the rich and the poor in a reasonable fashion. And without such a basis for conflict resolution, how could we flourish, as libertarians claim we would, under a minimal state?[24] For societies to flourish in this fashion, the libertarian ideal must resolve severe conflicts of interest in ways that it would be reasonable to require everyone affected to accept. But as we have seen, that requirement can be satisfied only if the rich sacrifice the liberty to meet their luxury needs so that the poor can have the liberty to meet their basic needs.

It should also be noted that this case for restricting the liberty of the rich depends upon the willingness of the poor to take advantage of whatever opportunities are available to them to engage in mutually beneficial work, so that failure of the poor to take advantage of such opportunities would normally cancel or at least significantly reduce the obligation of the rich to restrict their own liberty for the benefit of the poor.[25] In addition, the poor would be required to return the equivalent of any surplus possessions they have taken from the rich once they are able to do so and still satisfy their basic needs. And the poor would not be required to keep the liberty to which they are entitled. They could give up part or all of it or could risk losing it on the chance of gaining a greater share of liberties or other social goods.[26] Consequently, the case for restricting the liberty of the rich for the benefit of the poor is neither unconditional nor inalienable.

Now one might think that once the rich realize that the poor should have the liberty not to be interfered with when taking from the surplus possessions of the rich what they require to satisfy their basic needs, they should stop producing any surplus whatsoever. Yet this would be in their interest only if (a) the rich did not enjoy producing a surplus, (b) the recognition of the rightful claims of the poor would exhaust the surplus of the rich, and (c) the poor would never be in a position to be obligated to repay what they appropriated from the rich. Fortunately for the poor, all these conditions are unlikely to obtain. But suppose they did. Wouldn't the poor be justified in appropriating or threatening to appropriate even the non-surplus possessions of those who can produce more, in order to get them to do so? Surely this would not seem to be an unreasonable imposition on those who can produce more, because it would not seem to be unreasonable to require them to be more productive when the alternative is that the poor would, through no fault of their own, fail to meet their basic needs. And surely it would be unreasonable to require the poor to do anything less when their basic needs are at stake.

Nevertheless, it may be the case that those who can produce more can only bring themselves to do so if they can benefit themselves to a degree that requires the denial of the basic needs of at least some of the poor. And this could be the case even if the poor are in a position to appropriate or threaten to appropriate the nonsurplus possessions of those who can be more productive. In severe conflict situations like these, however, there simply is no moral resolution, that is, no resolution that it would be reasonable to require all parties to accept. As we noted before, such possibilities conflict with the libertarian assumption that societies can flourish under the limited constraints of a minimal state, because in order for this assumption to hold, the libertarian ideal must resolve severe conflicts of interest in ways that it would be reasonable to require everyone affected to accept. In cases of conflict, this requires that the rich and talented sacrifice the liberty to fulfill their need for luxury so that the poor and untalented can have the liberty to meet their basic needs.

This is an important conclusion in our assessment of the libertarian ideal, because it shows that ultimately the right of the poor to appropriate what they require to meet their basic needs does not depend, as many welfare liberals, like John Rawls, have thought, upon the talented having sufficient self-interested incentives to produce a surplus. All that is necessary is that the talented can produce a surplus and that the poor cannot meet their basic needs in any other way.

Of course, there will be cases in which the poor fail to satisfy their basic needs, not because of any direct restriction of liberty on the part of the rich, but because the poor are in such dire need that they are unable even to attempt to take from the rich what they require to meet their basic needs. In such cases, the rich would not be performing any act of commission that would prevent the poor from taking what they require. Yet even in such cases, the rich would normally be performing acts of commission that would prevent other persons from taking part of the rich's surplus possessions and using it to aid the poor. And when assessed from a moral point of view, restricting the liberty of these other persons would not be morally justified for the very same reason that restricting the liberty of the poor to meet their own basic needs would not be morally justified: it would not be reasonable to require all of those affected to accept such a restriction of liberty.

Let us now consider whether these same conclusions can be established against Lockean libertarians, who take a set of rights, typically including a right to life and a right to property, as basic and then interpret liberty as being unconstrained by other persons from doing what one has a right to do. According to this view, a right to life is understood as a right not to be treated unjustly, and a right to property is understood as a right to acquire goods and resources either by initial acquisition or by voluntary agreement. In order to evaluate this view, we must determine what is entailed by these rights.

Presumably, a right to life understood as a right not to be killed unjustly would not be violated by defensive measures designed to protect one's person from life-threatening attacks.[27] Yet would this right be violated when the rich prevent the poor from taking what they require to satisfy their basic nutritional needs? Obviously, as a consequence of such preventive actions, poor people sometimes do starve to death. Have the rich, then, in contributing to this result, killed the poor, or have they simply let them die; and, if they have killed the poor, have they done so unjustly?

Sometimes the rich, in preventing the poor from taking what they require to meet their basic nutritional needs, would not in fact be killing the poor but would only be causing them to be physically or mentally debilitated. Yet since such preventive acts involve resisting the life-preserving activities of the poor, when the poor do die as a consequence of such acts, it seems clear that the rich would be killing the poor, whether intentionally or unintentionally.

Of course, Lockean libertarians would want to argue that such killing is simply a consequence of the legitimate exercise of property rights and, hence, not unjust. But to understand why Lockean libertarians are mistaken in this regard, let us appeal again to those fundamental principles of morality, the "ought" implies "can" principle and the conflict resolution principle. In this context, these principles can be used to assess two opposing accounts of property rights. According to the first account, a right to property is not conditional upon whether other persons have sufficient opportunities and resources to satisfy their basic needs. This view holds that the initial acquisition and voluntary agreement of some can leave others, through no fault of their own, dependent upon charity for the satisfaction of their most basic needs. By contrast, according to the second account, initial acquisition and voluntary agreement can confer title of property on all goods and resources except those surplus goods and resources of the rich that are required to satisfy the basic needs of those poor who through no fault of their own lack opportunities and resources to satisfy their own basic needs.

Recall that there are two interpretations of the basic right to liberty on which the Spencerian view is grounded: one interpretation that ignores the liberty of the poor not to be interfered with when taking from the surplus possessions of the rich what they require to meet their basic needs, and the other, an interpretation that gives that liberty priority over the liberty of the rich not to be interfered with when using their surplus for luxury purposes. Here there are two interpretations of the right to property on which the Lockean view is grounded: one interpretation that regards the right to property as *not* conditional upon the resources and opportunities available to others, and one interpretation that regards the right to property as conditional upon the resources and opportunities available to others. And just as in the case of the Spencerian view, here we need to appeal to those fundamental principles of morality, the "ought" implies "can" principle and the conflict resolution principle, to decide which interpretation is morally acceptable.

It is clear that only the unconditional interpretation of property rights would generally justify the killing of the poor as a legitimate exercise of the property rights of the rich. Yet it would be unreasonable to require the poor to accept anything other than some version of the conditional interpretation of property rights. Moreover, according to the conditional interpretation, it does not matter whether the poor would actually die or are only physically or mentally debilitated as a result of such acts of prevention. Either result would preclude property rights from arising. Of course, the poor may have no real alternative to acquiescing to a political system modeled after the unconditional interpretation of property rights, even though such a system imposes an unreasonable sacrifice upon them—a sacrifice that we could not blame them for trying to evade. At the same time, although the rich would be disinclined to do so, it would not be unreasonable to require them to accept a political system modeled after the conditional interpretation of property rights—the interpretation favored by the poor. Consequently, if we assume that however else we specify the requirements of morality, they cannot violate the "ought" implies "can" principle and the conflict resolution principle, it follows that despite what Lockean libertarians claim, the right to life and the right to property endorsed by them actually support a right to welfare.

By a similar argument that weighs the conflicting liberties or rights involved, it can be shown that an ideal of liberty also supports a right to equal opportunity. Now it is possible that libertarians convinced to some extent by the above arguments might want to accept a right to welfare and a right to the basic opportunities that are necessary for the satisfaction of one's basic needs but then might want to deny a right to equal opportunity. Such a stance, however, is only plausible if we restrict the class of morally legitimate claimants to those within a given (affluent) society, for only then would a right to equal opportunity be different from the right to the opportunities necessary for the satisfaction of people's basic needs. But once it is recognized that the class of morally legitimate claimants includes distant peoples and future generations, then even libertarians should grant that guaranteeing the basic opportunities necessary for the satisfaction of their basic needs to all morally legitimate claimants would lead to providing them all with roughly equal opportunity.[28]

What these arguments show, therefore, is that a libertarian ideal supports the same practical requirements as a welfare liberal ideal. Both favor a right to welfare and a right to equal opportunity. Suppose, then, that a welfare liberal ideal of fairness, a libertarian ideal of liberty, a communitarian ideal of the common good, a feminist ideal of androgyny, and a socialist ideal of equality, when correctly interpreted, all can be shown to support a right to welfare and a right to equal opportunity. Since most people already accept one or another of these moral ideals, to make people moral, it should suffice to show them that these different ideals actually support the same practical requirements.

Of course, people suffering from weakness of will cannot be moved effectively by the force of argument alone to act in accord with even their deepest commitments, and I do not propose to show how this affliction can be overcome. My argument is simply directed to those people who can be counted on to act upon their deepest moral commitments once it becomes clear to them what these commitments practically require. These are the people I hope to make moral by the force of the argument I have sketched.

Notes

1. See Knud Rasmussen, *The People of the Polar North* (London: Kegan Paul, Trench, Trubner & Co., 1908), pp. 106–111; and Peter Freuchen, *Book of the Eskimos* (New York: World Publishing Co., 1961), pp. 193–206. And cf. Hans Reusch, *Top of the World* (New York: Pocket Books, 1951), pp. 123–26.

2. See Mary Douglas, *Purity and Danger: An Analysis of Concepts of Pollution and Taboo* (London: Routledge & Kegan Paul, 1966), p. 39.

3. "Ought" presupposes "can" here. Unless the members of the society have the capacity to entertain and follow both self-interested and moral reasons for acting, it does not make any sense asking whether they ought or ought not to do so.

4. For an account of what counts as *relevant* self-interested or moral reasons, see James P. Sterba, *How to Make People Just: A Practical Reconciliation of Alternative Conceptions of Justice* (Totowa, N.J.: Roman & Littlefield, 1988), pp. 165–66.

5. For a discussion of the causal links involved here, see U.S. House Subcommittee of International Economic Policy and Trade of the Committee on Foreign Affairs, *Marketing and Promotion of Infant Formula in Developing Countries: Hearing before the Subcommittee of International Economic Policy and Trade of the Committee on Foreign Affairs*, 96th Cong., 2d sess., 1980. See also Maggie McComas and others, *The Dilemma of Third World Nutrition* (n.p.: Nestle, 1983).

6. Assume that both jobs have the same beneficial effects on the interests of others.

7. I am assuming that acting contrary to reason is an important failing with respect to the requirements of reason, and that there are many ways of not acting in (perfect) accord with reason that do not constitute acting contrary to reason.

8. Otherwise, they would really fall under the classification of aesthetic reasons.

9. Of course, such reasons would have to be taken into account at some point in a complete justification for morality, but the method of integrating such reasons into a complete justification of morality

would simply parallel the method already used for integrating self-interested and altruistic reasons.

10. This is because morality itself already represents a compromise between egoism and altruism. So to ask that moral reasons be weighed against self-interested reasons is, in effect, to count self-interested reasons twice—once in the compromised view between egoism and altruism, and then again when moral reasons are weighed against self-interested reasons. But to count self-interested reasons twice is clearly objectionable.

11. Assume that all these methods of waste disposal have roughly the same amount of beneficial effects on the interests of others.

12. Kai Nielson, "Why Should I be Moral? Revisited," *American Philosophical Quarterly* 1, no. 21 (January 1984): 90.

13. Of course, there are people who cannot be altruists or moralists but only egoists. For such people, there is no question about their being required to act morally or altruistically. But the interesting philosophical question is not about such people but about people, like ourselves, who are capable of acting morally, egoistically, or altruistically and are seeking a rational justification for following one course of action over others.

14. Kurt Baier, *The Moral Point of View* (New York: Random House, 1965), p. 150.

15. I have argued for this conclusion in *How To Make People Just*.

16. Each of these approaches faces certain difficulties. The principal difficulty with the first approach is that unless one arbitrarily restricts what is to count as an interference, conflicting liberties will abound, particularly in all areas of social life. The principal difficulty with the second approach is that as long as a person's rights have not been violated, his or her liberty has not have been restricted either, even if that person is kept in prison for the rest of his or her days. I do not propose to try to decide between these two approaches. Later in this section, I argue that on either approach, the libertarian ideal can be practically reconciled with a welfare liberal ideal.

17. Isaiah Berlin, *Four Essays on Liberty* (London and New York: Oxford University Press, 1969), pp. xxviii–xl.

18. On this point, see Maurice Cranston, *Freedom: A New Analysis* (New York: Longmans, Green, 1953), pp. 52–53; Crawford Brough Macpherson, *Democratic Theory: Essays in Retrieval* (Oxford: Oxford University Press, 1973), pp. 95–96; Joel Feinberg, *Rights, Justice, and the Bounds of Liberty* (Princeton: Princeton University Press, 1980), chapter 1.

19. It is not being assumed here that the surplus possessions of

the rich are either justifiably or unjustifiably possessed by the rich. Moreover, according to Spencerian libertarians, it is an assessment of the liberties involved that determines whether the possession is justifiable or not.

20. See John Hospers, *Libertarianism* (Los Angeles: Nash Publishers, 1971), chapter 7; and Tibor R. Machan, *Human Rights and Human Liberties* (Chicago: Nelson Hall, 1975), pp. 231–22.

21. See Alvin Goldman, *A Theory of Human Action* (Englewood Cliffs, N.J.: Prentice-Hall, 1970), pp. 208–15; and William Frankena, "Obligation and Ability," in *Philosophical Analysis*, ed. Max Black (Ithaca, N.Y.: Cornell University Press, 1950), pp. 157–75. One might think that the "ought" implies "can" principle would be useful only for illustrating moral conflicts rather than resolving them. But this is only true if one interprets the "can" principle to exclude only "what a person lacks the power to do." If one interprets the "can" to exclude, in addition, "what would involve so great a sacrifice that it would be unreasonable to ask the person to do," then the principle can be used to resolve moral conflicts as well as to state them. Libertarians would not object to this broader interpretation of the "ought" implies "can" principle, since they do not ground their claim to liberty on the existence of irresolvable moral conflicts.

This broader interpretation of the "ought" implies "can" principle is also a natural extension of the narrower interpretation of the principle. For while the narrower interpretation excludes from the domain of obligation actions that are logically, physiologically, and psychologically impossible to perform, the broader interpretation excludes as well actions that are morally impossible because it is contrary to reason to ask people to do them. It would also be a mistake to reject this broader interpretation of the "ought" implies "can" principle on grounds of egoism, as some libertarians might want to do.

I first appealed to the broad interpretation of the "ought" implies "can" principle given in this chapter to bring libertarians around to the practical requirements of welfare liberalism in an expanded version of an article entitled "Neo-Libertarianism," *American Philosophical Quarterly* 15 (April 1978): 115–21. In 1982, T. M. Scanlon in "Contractualism and Utilitarianism," in *Utilitarianism and Beyond*, ed. Sen Amartya and others (London: Cambridge University Press, 1982), pp. 103–28, appealed to much the same standard to arbitrate the debate between contractarians and utilitarians. In my judgment, however, this standard embedded in the "ought" implies "can" principle can be more effectively used in the debate with libertarians than in the debate with utilitarians, because sacrifices libertarians standardly seek to impose on the less advantaged are more outrageous and, hence, more easily shown to be contrary to reason.

22. See Sterba, "Is There a Rationale for Punishment?" *American Journal of Jurisprudence* 29 (1984): 29–43.

23. By the liberty of the rich to meet their luxury needs, I continue to mean the liberty of the rich not to be interfered with when using their surplus possessions for luxury purposes. Similarly, by the liberty of the poor to meet their basic needs, I continue to mean the liberty of the poor not to be interfered with when taking what they require to meet their basic needs from the surplus possessions of the rich.

24. As further evidence, notice that those libertarians who justify a minimal state do so on grounds that such a state would arise from reasonable disagreements concerning the application of libertarian rights. They do not justify the minimal state on the grounds that it would be needed to keep in submission large numbers of people who could not come to see the reasonableness of those rights.

25. The employment opportunities offered to the poor must be honorable and supportive of self-respect. To do otherwise would be to offer the poor the opportunity to meet some of their basic needs at the cost of denying some of their other basic needs.

26. The poor cannot, however, give up the liberty to which their children are entitled.

27. See Sterba, "Moral Approaches to Nuclear Strategy: A Critical Evaluation," *Canadian Journal of Philosophy*, 12, supp. 12 (1986): 75–109.

28. For the argument, see Sterba, "The Welfare Rights of Distant Peoples and Future Generations: Moral Side-Constraints on Social Policy," *Social Theory and Practice* 7 (spring 1981): 99–119.

5

Animal Rights, Egalitarianism, and Nihilism

Louis P. Pojman

The racist violates the principle of equality by giving greater weight to the interests of members of his own race when there is a clash between their interests and the interests of those of another race. The sexist violates the principle of equality by favoring the interests of his own sex. Similarly the speciesist allows the interests of his own species to override the greater interests of members of other species. The pattern is identical in each case.

—Peter Singer, *Animal Liberation*

There is no fundamental difference between man and the higher animals.

—Charles Darwin, *The Descent of Man*

Introduction: A Description of the Problem

What is the problem concerning the moral status of animals? Just this: on the one hand, we normally regard human beings as possessing high intrinsic worth, dignity. We say with Kant that humans, qua rational beings, are ends in themselves and may not be used as mere means for the good of others. We affirm with our founding fathers that "these truths are self-evident, that all" humans are equal and possess "certain inalienable rights, that among these are life, liberty, and the pursuit of happiness." We hold with Rawls that people have equal dignity, so that not even the utilitarian good can override these basic rights.

On the other hand, our growing understanding of evolutionary biology leads us to believe that the similarities (common physical properties) between some primates and humans turn out to be greater than the differences. The absolute gap thesis, which posits a clear axiological distinction between humans and other animals, is false. As Darwin said, "There is no fundamental difference between man and the higher animals." We are essentially animals. Whereas our forebears judged humans as occupying an axiological space between angels and animals, some contemporary views put us between the animal and the computer, as reasonably accurate, conscious calculators.

Now put these two propositions together. Since we have intrinsic or inherent worth and since animals—at least mammals, such as cetaceans (for example, whales, dolphins, and porpoises), primates (for example, chimpanzees and monkeys), and pigs, dogs, cats, elephants, cows, horses, rats, rabbits, and mice—are relevantly similar to us, these mammals must also have intrinsic worth. Since intrinsic worth yields basic civil rights, higher animals must be treated with the respect usually accorded to humans. We must recognize that they possess natural rights, including the right of life, the right not to be harmed, and the right of liberty. It follows, given suitable supporting premises, that our present practices of eating meat, hunting, and animal experimentation—practices based on the absolute gap thesis—are morally wrong.

This is the heart of the animal rights argument. It begins with the egalitarian thesis, what Tom Regan has called "a consensus view in philosophy," that all adult humans are of equal worth, and it proceeds to show that the implications of this thesis lead to viewing animals as having equal positive worth, animal or mammal egalitarianism.[1] Since humans have equal rights, it follows that animals have them as well.

In this chapter, I primarily use the term *rights* to cover the idea of natural rights, the idea that certain natural properties in animals give them special moral consideration, cause them to have claims over and against us. This is a different theory from that which views rights as simply correlative to duties, which denies that a being has rights but affirms that we still have duties to those creatures. For example, if I have a duty to some being B, then B has a right against me, whether B can claim it or not. So in this weaker sense of rights, flowing from deontic ("ought") language, we can speak of animals having rights even if we do not want to accept a stronger view of natural rights. My arguments are mainly leveled against the stronger thesis, although they are applicable to Singer's version of the weaker thesis.

In what follows I shall set forth seven theories of the moral status of animals: three that grant them little or no status, one that grants them substantial but not equal status, and three that grant them some kind of equal status with ourselves. My primary goal in this chapter is to consider various versions of the egalitarian animal rights argument, especially those of Peter Singer, Tom Regan, and Paul Taylor, in order to determine whether these radical versions entail moral nihilism, the thesis that we have no moral duties at all. I answer that they do indeed. In the briefer, second part of the chapter, I outline a way out of the problem into which the egalitarian systems lead us.

Seven Theories of the Moral Status of Animals

Seven theories on the moral status of animals appear in the history of Western philosophy and religion, from assigning animals no status on the one extreme to assigning them equal status with humans on the other extreme.

The No Status Theory

The no status theory was set forth by René Descartes (1596–1650), who held that an absolute gap exists between animals and human beings. Unlike humans, animals have no rights or moral status because they have no souls. Since, according to Descartes, the soul is necessary to consciousness, animals cannot feel pain or pleasure. They are mere machines. Their superiority over man-made machines derives from their source. "From this aspect the body is regarded as a machine which, having been made by the hands of God, is incomparably better arranged, and possesses in itself movements which are much more admirable than any of those which can be invented by man."[2]

According to Descartes, animals are automata who move and bark and utter sounds like well-wound clocks. Because they lack a soul, which is the locus of consciousness and value, they have no moral status whatsoever. It is no more morally wrong to pull the ears off a dog or eat a cow than it is to kick a stone or eat a carrot.

In Descartes's time animals were subjected to excruciating tortures in physiological experiments. Dogs were restrained by nailing their paws to boards so that they could be more easily observed while being cut open. Sometimes their vocal chords were cut so that their shrieks would not disturb the anatomists. In the next century Nicholas Fontaine observed the following: "[The anatomists] administered beatings to dogs with perfect indifference, and made fun of those who pitied the creatures as if they felt pain. They said the animals were clocks; that the cries they emitted when struck were only the noise of a little spring that had been touched, but that the whole body was without feeling. They nailed poor animals up on boards by their four paws to vivisect them and see the circulation of the blood, which was a great subject of conversation."[3]

We now know that Descartes and the anatomists were wrong. Higher animals, having a similar nervous system to our own, do feel pain and pleasure. They have consciousness and engage in purposeful behavior. Dogs and cats manifest intelligence; gorillas and chimpanzees exhibit complex abstracting and reasoning abilities and appear to communicate through language. The differences between humans and other animals are more a matter of degree than of kind.

Although implausible in the extreme, the Cartesian view still has advocates. I have heard it defended by hunters and owners of animal factories. Witness the words of Roy Johnson in the trapper's journal *Trapline Ramblings*. "If a man beats his wife every day, she suffers because she has an immortal soul. But if he beats his hound-dog, it may yelp some but it won't suffer because it has no soul." And again, in a book sponsored by the fur industry, *Animals and Men—Past, Present, and Future*, we read the testimony of a hunter: "I have the impression, based on field observation, that many shot animals do not especially show feelings of pain. There are no 'rights' in the natural world—to the victor belongs the spoils. It is hard to know what people mean by 'cruel' or 'inhumane'."[4]

This view is also reflected in Nobel Prize-winning molecular biologist David Baltimore's claim that no moral issue is involved in animal research, and in the writings of psychologists, G. Gallup and S. D. Suarez, who write that "the evolution of moral and ethical behavior in man may be such that it is not applicable to other species." Similarly, the veterinarian F. S. Jacobs writes that "domestic animals exist in this world because they fulfill man's needs. . . . Therefore it is meaningless to speak of their rights to existence, because they would not exist if man did not exist."[5]

One advantage of extreme speciesism that has not often been mentioned is its simplicity. It is relatively easy to identify members of a species. To have a clear demarcation between humans and nonhumans saves us from a great deal of worry. It is cost-effective to hold this line clear, for the destruction of the species partition opens the way for ambiguity and uncertainty. Problems arise, such as when do human needs or interests override those of nonhuman animals? What is a basic versus a nonbasic need or interest? What is the relative value of a human versus a chimpanzee, a dog, a mouse, or a cockroach? A new casuistry is called for, where the doctrine of absolute difference was once a secure settlement.

The Minimal Status Theory

The nineteenth-century British philosopher William Whewell seems to have held a somewhat less radical view of animals than Descartes, for Whewell does not deny that animals have feelings, only that we have obligation to enhance their pleasure. "The pleasures of animals are elements of a very different order from the pleasures of man. We are bound to endeavor to augment the pleasures of men, not only because they are pleasures, but because they are human pleasures. We are bound to men by the universal tie of humanity, of human brotherhood. We have no such tie to animals."[6]

The nineteenth-century British philosopher Philip Austin adds that while we have no positive duties to animals, we ought not to be cruel to them. "Animals should be treated with personal indifference; they should not be petted, they should not be ill-treated. It should always be remembered that they are our slaves, not our equals, and for this reason it is well to keep up such practices as hunting and fishing, driving and riding, merely to demonstrate in a practical way man's dominion."[7] Perhaps this minimalist view should be called the slave status theory, for so long as we do not purposefully torture animals, we may use them however we wish. Since they have no inherent value, they are not to be taken into consideration in any utilitarian calculus.

Philosophers like Stephen Stitch and R. G. Frey acknowledge that animals do feel pain and pleasure, but they deny that animals can be said to have interests or beliefs.[8] Frey argues that rights are predicated upon beliefs and interests, and since animals fail to have these, they fail to possess rights. In order to have a belief, one must be able to conceptualize and entertain a proposition or sentence, but there is no evidence that animals can do this. In order to have interests, according to Frey, one must be able to have desires, but desires also involve propositional content, beliefs, and this is something that animals do not possess. Since only beings with interests can have rights, it follows that animals do not have rights.

Animals may not have rights, but Stitch and Frey's arguments are not compelling. First, animals, such as dogs, chimpanzees, and gorillas have memories of where they have placed objects. For example, at mealtime Fido scratches at the door to the next room. His master interprets that to mean that Fido wants him to open the door so that he (Fido) can fetch his meaty bone. This hypothesis is confirmed when the master opens the door and watches Fido make a dash to a heap of paper at the corner of the room from which Fido procures a meaty bone. There is no consensus of the correct analysis of human beliefs, but whatever beliefs are, they seem functionally equivalent with what causes Fido to scratch on the door and make a dash for the stack of papers in the corner of the room. His behavior is intentional, if any behavior is. Second, there seems no good reason for withholding the concept of interests from animals. Having food, water, sleep, and a comfortable dwelling is in an animal's interest, just as these items are normally in a human animal's interest.

Finally, another type of minimalist view is the contractarian doctrine that animals are not seriously morally considerable since they are not bargainers in the social contract. We should not do unnecessary harm to animals, but it is a misapplication of the idea of rights to apply such a property to them. The only moral principle that applies to animals is "*Primum non nocere*" (the first thing [is] to do no harm), interpreted as a prima facie rule—do no unjustified harm to animals. Some would place the Judeo-Christian view of animals in this category, but I think it belongs in the next one.

The Indirect Obligation Theory

The dominant position in Western philosophy and religion has been the view that while animals have no inherent rights, we ought to treat them kindly. Why? Because they are the property of others who do have moral rights. We have indirect duties to dumb animals because we have direct obligations to rational beings, God, and other people who own them.

The creation story of Genesis supports a stewardship model of creation. Animals and the rest of nature are God's property, loaned to humanity for our good use, which we are obligated to cultivate and protect for God's sake. "And God blessed them [man and woman] and God said to them, 'Be fruitful and multiply, and fill the earth and subdue it; and have dominion over the fish of the sea and over the birds of the air and over every living thing that moves upon the earth.' And God said, 'Behold, I have given you every plant yielding seed which is upon the face of all the earth, and every tree with seed in its fruit; you shall have them for food.' "[9]

Thomas Aquinas (1225–74) and Immanuel Kant (1724–1804) hold that cruelty to animals is wrong because it forms bad character and leads to cruelty to human beings. Aquinas holds to a hierarchical view that obligates humans to use animals for human good.

> There is no sin in using a thing for the purpose for which it is. Now the order of things is such that the imperfect are for the perfect . . . thing, like plants which merely have life, are all alike for animals, and all animals are for man. Wherefore it is not unlawful if men use plants for the good of animals, and animals for the good of man, as the Philosopher [Aristotle] states.
>
> Now the most necessary use would seem to consist in the fact that animals use plants, and men use animals, for food, and this cannot be done unless these be deprived of life, wherefore it is lawful both to take life from plants for the use of animals and animals for the use of men. In fact this is in keeping with the commandment of God himself (Genesis 1:29, 30 and Genesis 9:3).[10]

Aquinas goes on to say that we do have indirect obligations to animals, for the way we treat them will doubtless spill over into the way we treat fellow humans. "If any passages of Holy Writ seem to forbid us to be cruel to dumb animals, for instance to kill a bird with its young: this is either to remove man's thoughts from being cruel to other men, and lest through being cruel to animals one become cruel to human beings: or because injury to an animal leads to the temporal hurt of man, either of the doer of the deed, or of another." [11]

Similarly, Kant argues that we have "no direct duties" to animals, for they "are not self-conscious and are there merely as a means to an end."

> The end is man. . . . Our duties towards animals are merely indirect duties towards humanity. Animal nature has analogies to human nature, and by doing our duties to animals in respect to manifestations of human nature, we indirectly do our duty to humanity. . . . If a man shoots his dog because the animal is no longer capable of service, he does not fail in his duty to the dog, for the dog cannot judge, but his act is inhuman and damages in itself that humanity which it is his duty to show towards mankind. If he is not to stifle his human feelings, he must practice kindness towards animals, for he who is cruel to animals becomes hard also in his dealing with men. [12]

The weakness of the indirect obligation theory is that it makes rational self-consciousness the sole criterion for being morally considerable. While such self-consciousness may be the criterion for having full-blooded rights and for being a morally responsible agent, it is not the only thing that is of moral importance. Pain and suffering are bad in themselves, and we have duties both to refrain from causing these things and to ameliorate and eliminate them.

Moderate Egalitarianism: The Equal Consideration Theory

The equal consideration theory was first set forth by Jeremy Bentham (1748–1832), the father of classical utilitarianism, and was developed by Peter Singer in his epoch-making book *Animal Liberation* (1976). Utilitarianism is a nonspeciesist, egalitarian moral theory in which animals are given an equal vote with humans. Bentham's egalitarian dictum "Each to count for one, no one for more than one," applies to all sentient creatures regardless of species and takes the pleasures and pains of each individual, whether a mouse or a human, equally into consideration, weighing them in the hedonic calculus. Each pain (evil) and pleasure (good) is measured according to its intensity, duration, certainty, nearness, fecundity, and purity. We then are to "sum up all the values of all the pleasures on the one side, and those of all the pains on the other. The balance, if it be on the side of pleasure, will give the good tendency of the act upon the whole, with respect to the interests of that individual person; if on the side of pain, the bad tendency of it upon the whole." Pain being equated with the evil and pleasure with the good, the goal of moral action is to produce the optimal aggregate balance of pleasure over pain. In a classic passage, Bentham compares the irrationality of our views toward animals with the irrationality of our views toward other races.

> The day *may come*, when the rest of the animal creation may acquire those rights which never could have been withholden from them but by the hand of tyranny. The French have already discovered that the blackness of the skin is no reason why a human being should be abandoned without redress to the caprice of a tormentor. It may come one day to be recognized that the number of the legs [or] the villosity of the skin are reasons equally insufficient for abandoning a sensitive being to the same fate. What else is it that should trace the insuperable line? Is it the faculty of reason, or, perhaps, the faculty of discourse? But a full-grown horse or dog is beyond comparison a more rational, as well as a more conversable animal, than an infant of a day, or a week, or even a month, old. But suppose the case were otherwise, what would it avail? The question is not, Can they *reason*? not, Can they *talk*? but, Can they *suffer*?[13]

Bentham's hedonic act utilitarianism has been subject to two hundred years of cogent and familiar criticism. I have criticized his doctrines elsewhere,[14] so I must be content merely to note some of the salient objections. First, the hedonic calculus (intensity, duration, certainty, and so forth) is unworkable, since only God could specify values to the various variables in individual cases. How do you compare two humans suffering a toothache, let alone a dog and a human? Second, its hedonic aspect seems so crude as to deserve the epithet "pig philosophy," since it reduces all good to quantitative pleasure and evil to quantitative pain. Better a pig satisfied than Socrates dissatisfied! In a well-known experiment on rats by Olds, electrodes are wired to the limbic areas of the rat's brain. The rats are shown a button that, when pressed, will stimulate a reward or pleasure center in the brain. The rats in the experiment become addicted to the need for the stimulation, so that they lose interest in food and sex and spend most of their time pressing the stimulation button until they die. If the maximization of pleasure is what morality is all about, we ought to plug everyone, animals and humans, into these pleasure machines.

If Bentham's reductive hedonism is the sum of morality, then it would be morally right for five sadists who receive a total of 100 *hedons* in the process to torture a child who only suffers 50 *dolors* (antihedons). Or if a burglar will get more pleasure from my artwork than I do, he has a duty to steal it. If taking everyone's aggregate pleasure/pain into consideration would yield such an act as killing your innocent mother, your duty would be to kill her. The usual utilitarian response to such examples is that the bad side effects would make such dastardly acts disutile, but we can counter that response by saying either that even with the side effects the net effect would be maximal pleasure or that the killing would be a secret. A drug is given that would induce a heart attack and leave no trace of itself.

Sometimes utilitarians like Bentham, as in the passage above, and others I have heard arguing, speak as though the single concern of morality is to eliminate suffering in the world. If this were morality's only concern, or if we decided that the future would yield an aggregate balance of pain over pleasure (which is not implausible, given the amount of suffering in the world), we would have an obligation to eliminate all sentient life as painlessly as possible, since the only way to eliminate suffering (even gratuitous suffering) is to kill every living organism.

Peter Singer (like Mill before him), aware of the profound difficulties of classical utilitarianism—that it reduces moral reasoning to a crude and unworkable hedonic calculus in which agents are mere pain/pleasure receptacles—has attempted to set forth a more sophisticated version of utilitarianism. Singer's theory is a type of preference utilitarianism in which an act is moral if, and only if, it satisfies the highest aggregate of preferences. An act contrary to the preference of any being is wrong, unless it is outweighed by a stronger contrary preference. Three further theses are set forth, yielding a comprehensive ethic and including global duties to animals.

The first thesis concerns the principle of equality: every sentient being deserves to have his or her interests (that is, desires) given equal consideration. Singer rejects the Judeo-Christian notion that human beings have equal inherent value, and he instead bases the equality principle upon our capacity to have preferences. "Equality is a moral idea, not an assertion of fact. There is no logically compelling reason for assuming that a factual difference in ability between two people justifies any difference in the amount of consideration we give their needs and interests. *The principle of equality of human beings is not a description of an alleged actual equality among humans: it is a prescription of how we should treat humans.*"[15]

Appealing to Bentham's dictum, each sentient being is to count for one and only for one. Status and privilege should play no part in doling out benefits. Rather, we should distribute goods on the basis of need and desire. The interests of everyone affected by an action should be taken into account and given the same weight as the like interests of any other being.

The second thesis is that since speciesism constitutes a violation of the principle of equality, it must be rejected. Singer compares speciesism, the arbitrary favoring of one's species, with racism. "The racist . . . [gives] greater weight to the interests of members of his own race, when there is a clash between their interests and the interests of another race. . . . Similarly the speciesist allows the interests of his own species to override the greater interests of members of other species."[16]

Suffering is suffering no matter whose it is. If a dog and

a child are in equal pain and we have only a single pain reliever, it is not obvious who should get it. If the dog is in greater pain, the dog should. If the child is in greater pain, the child should. Singer asks, "What, for instance, are we to do about genuine conflicts of interest like rats biting slum children? I am not sure of the answer, but the essential point is just we *do* see this as a conflict of interest, that we recognize that rats have interests too."[17]

The third thesis, emphasizing the importance of self-consciousness, maintains that there is a difference between our equal ability to suffer and our equal worth as rational, self-conscious agents. Here Singer separates himself from Bentham, who simply compares pleasures and pains. Singer argues that rational self-consciousness has a deep effect on how and what we desire, over and above mere sentience. Sentience, or the ability to suffer, gives us a baseline equality for some, but not all, considerations.

The difference between Singer and Bentham is revealed in Singer's discussion of killing. Whereas for Benthamite classical utilitarianism, "there is no direct significance in the fact that a person's desires for the future go unfulfilled when he or she is killed," Singer argues that a self-conscious person possesses a concept of himself as a distinct individual with a definite past and a future, who is "capable of having desires about its own future."

> For example, a professor of philosophy may hope to write a book demonstrating the objective nature of ethics; a student may look forward to graduating; a child may want to go for a ride in an airplane. To take the life of these people, without their consent, is to thwart the victim's desires for the future, in a way that killing a snail or a day-old infant presumably is not. It is not arbitrary to hold that the life of a self-aware being, . . . capable of abstract thought, of planning for the future, of complex acts of communication, and so on, is more valuable than the life of a being without these capacities.[18]

We may distinguish between those activities that cause suffering and those that cause death. It may be worse to cause animals to suffer than to kill them, since the latter may be done with minimum pain and the animal generally does not have an understanding of life and death. With humans the situation is just the reverse. Since humans generally prefer life with pain (up to a limit) to death, it is worse to kill humans than to cause them suffering.

Even though humans in general possess capacities that merit special consideration in some areas, this fact becomes irrelevant when it comes to suffering. In suffering we are to be given equal consideration. Since sentience lies at the core of our moral thinking, and language and intelligence lie at the periphery, a large part of our morality will have to do with liberating people and animals from suffering.

The outcome of this theory is that we ought to become vegetarians and do everything in our power to end the harmful torture factories in which animals are raised and prepared for human consumption. Furthermore, we ought to curtail the vast majority of scientific research on animals that promotes unjustified suffering. Finally, we should end most hunting and trapping, such as trapping animals for fur.

Although Singer's views on the prejudice of speciesism compel us to rethink the moral status of animals, they still have problems. First, let me point out that his theory does not yield the results that he wants: vegetarianism, the end of animal factories, and a moratorium of all but the most urgent animal experiments. At least it is not obvious that Singer has made a convincing case against these practices. The Achilles' heel in his argument is the idea of *preference*. How does Singer know that the abolition of factory farms will result in a net gain of preference satisfaction? Imagine the suffering that would be incurred by such abolition. Besides our losing the delicious taste of meat in our diet (which by itself might not outweigh the animals' plight), hundreds of thousands of factory farm workers, transporters, business owners, and butchers would be unemployed. Their families would suffer. Social chaos might ensue. How do we weigh the preferences of all these self-conscious persons against the preferences of chickens, pigs, and cows? Perhaps, as R. G. Frey has argued, the utilitarian thing to do would be to work for reforms in the factory farms, permitting animals more space, exercise, and pleasure.[19]

Furthermore, even if we should take steps, gradual or sudden, to end the factory farm system, my becoming a vegetarian will not make a notable difference. If I alone cease eating meat, probably not one less pig or chicken will be raised for consumption, so that my suffering the loss of the taste of meat will yield a net disvalue in the scheme of things. Besides, meat eaters, simply by devouring more meat themselves, could always nullify any move on the part of vegetarians to create a positive situation. For example, suppose that 10,000 students and faculty suddenly decide to become vegetarians, thus saving 10,000 veal calves in a year and making it uneconomical for Old McDonald's Factory Farm to continue. Suppose the loss of the taste of meat adds up to 10,000 preference points and the closing of one animal factory results in 1,000,000 preference points. The utilitarian thing to do by a factor of 100 would be to become a vegetarian. But not necessarily. All the members of the Meat Lovers of America have to do is to eat more meat this year, so that McDonald's stays open and we vegetarians end up with a minus aggregate preference balance. By utilitarian standards, because we have deprived ourselves of preference satisfaction (10,000 preference units) for no reason, we have been immoral.

But there is a deeper problem with Singer's preference act utilitarianism that resides in the very notion of preference itself. For Singer the morally right act is the one that yields the highest preference satisfaction. No doubt, an animal's desire not to suffer outweighs my desire for the taste of meat, but this does not bring us to the conclusion that preferences should be considered equally or that preference maximization is the only relevant criterion to be considered.

Even if a dog is suffering more pain than a child, it is, nevertheless, deeply counterintuitive to say that we have a duty to give the single pain reliever to the dog. If the child is my child, then I think I have a strong duty to give it to him or her—even if the dog is my dog. The utilitarian might respond that this may be true because the child will live longer than the dog and have painful memories of the pain for a longer time.

Well, then imagine that it is an elderly man who is not likely to live longer than the puppy. I still sense that it would be right (or at least not wrong) to give the pill to the elderly man.

In fact, it seems to me that I should prefer my grandfather's vital interests more than the preferences of all the dogs in the world. If my grandfather were in danger of losing a leg and forty dogs were each in danger of losing a leg, and I could either save my grandfather's leg or all of the legs of the forty dogs, I would not hesitate to operate on grandfather. No matter how many dogs' legs I could save, I would feel it my duty to save grandfather's.

Singer, of course, might argue that this only proves that I am still an immoral speciesist. Isolated intuitions prove nothing. And so they do not. So let us proceed further.

Suppose that ten people will inherit my grandmother's vast wealth. Each has a strong preference that my grandmother die so they can pay their bills. The total of their preference units is 1,000. Suppose my grandmother's desire to continue to live is only 900 units. Wouldn't I—supposing that I, as a utilitarian, can pull it off without too much guilt—have a duty to kill grandmother as painlessly as possible?

"No," the preference utilitarian exclaims. "For you have forgotten the unintended side effects of creating fear in the minds of others that this might be done to them and so magnifying the negative preference points."

Well, then, all I have to do is be pretty sure that the poison I administer to grandmother's tea, which induces a heart attack, is the kind that leaves no trace.

In fact, can't the preference utilitarian do anything he or she wants, including killing people, taking their property, and breaking promises to them, just so long as his or her preference (or the aggregate preferences of his group) outweigh the preference of the victim? If you suddenly become despondent and no longer value life, why can't I utilitarianly kill you if it satisfies a preference to do so? If I can get you to care less than you do about your Mercedes Benz and can ensure that only minimal bad side effects will follow, can I not steal your car with complete utilitarian approval?

Perhaps you would reply that this would be exploitation. Well, why is exploitation wrong? If I desire to exploit you more than you dislike being exploited, doesn't my preference win out over yours?

Likewise, couldn't we justify slavery just by brainwashing the slaves to prefer slavery to freedom or at least not to value freedom more than we value having slaves?

In the end, Singer's argument does not gain any advantage over Bentham's crude hedonic calculus. It is simply that instead of people being *pleasure/pain* receptacles, they now become *preference* receptacles.

Finally, it turns out that Singer's principle of equality is not really about equality at all. Self-consciousness gives higher animals more consideration than merely sentient ones. The principle of equality is merely the rule of impartiality: apply your principles in a disinterested manner, according to the relevant criteria, not according to irrelevant ones. In the words of Aristotle, "Treat equals equally, and unequals unequally." It is purely a formal principle without any substantive force, one that could be used (as it was by Aristotle) to justify slavery and to justify the secret killing of innocents. It is compatible with Nietzche's Superman with his magnificent will (read "preference") for power.

To conclude, Singer's preference utilitarianism gets us no further than classical utilitarianism. It fails in particular to give a strong argument for vegetarianism or the abolition of animal factories. And it fails as a theory to establish the kind of equal consideration of interests at which he aims. But attempts have been made to salvage the essential core of Singer's program in an interspecies compromise. To this we now turn.

Weak Anthropocentrism: The Split Level Theory

The split level theory is found in the work of Martin Benjamin, Donald VanDeVeer, Louis Lombardi, and Mary Anne Warren.[20] It aims at correcting the positions I have discussed so far. The Cartesian no status theory, the minimal status theory, and the indirect obligation theory contain the insight that rational self-consciousness endows human beings with special worth, but they err on two counts: (1) in holding that animals do not have this quality at all (we know now that some do to some extent), and (2) in holding that only rational self-consciousness gives one any rights, or makes one morally considerable. At the other extreme, the equal consideration theory and, even more radical, the equal status theory (see the next section of this chapter) recognize the importance of sentience and the ability to suffer as morally considerable, but these views tend to neglect the aspect of rational self-consciousness as setting the majority of humans apart from the majority of animals.

The split level theory combines the insights of both types of theories. It is nonspeciesist in that it recognizes that some animals, such as chimpanzees and dolphins, may have an element of rational self-consciousness and that some humans may lack it (say, fetuses, babies, and senile or severely retarded people). The split level theory recognizes that both sentience and rational self-consciousness are important in working out a global interspecies morality. This view rejects Singer's equal consideration of interests principle. Rational self-consciousness does make a difference. A higher sort of being does emerge with humanity (and perhaps some higher primates and dolphins), so that we ought to treat humans with special respect.

This theory distinguishes between trivial needs and important needs. It says that with regard to important needs, human needs override animal needs, but animal's important needs override human trivial needs. For example, the need for sustenance and the need not to be harmed are important needs, whereas the need for having our tastes satisfied is a trivial need. So while humans have the right to kill animals if animals are necessary for health or life, we do not have the right to kill higher animals simply to satisfy our tastes. If there are equally good ways of finding nourishment, then humans have an obligation to seek those ways and permit animals to live unmolested.

This argument applies to higher animals who have a highly developed nervous system, enabling them to suffer and develop a sense of consciousness. Since there is no evidence that termites or mosquitoes have a sense of self, it is permissible to exterminate the termites and kill the mosquitoes when they threaten our interests. If we suddenly discovered that termites and mosquitoes were highly self-conscious, we would be obliged to act differently, but until we have evidence to that effect, we may continue our present practices.

Although the split level theory seems commonsensical, it needs a supporting argument. The clearest attempt at such an argument is given by Louis Lombardi in his article "Inherent Worth, Respect and Rights." Lombardi argues that while all animals have inherent worth, some have superior inherent worth. Inherent worth is tied up with a being's possessing valuable kinds (rather than degrees) of capacities. Human beings have the capacity for moral agency, which while it may not be superior to the other kinds of capacities, is, nevertheless, an additional type of capacity. Having this greater range of capacities endows humans with superior inherent worth. We might set forth the argument this way:

> 1. Animals and humans are different types of living things.
> 2. These types are differentiated by the range of their capacities as individuals.
> 3. The greater the range of an individual's capacity, the higher the degree of its inherent worth.
> 4. Humans have all (or most of) the basic capacities that animals have and significant additional ones besides.
> 5. Therefore, humans are of more inherent worth than animals.

There are several problems with Lombardi's argument. First, Lombardi's distinction between a kind of capacity and a degree of that capacity is made to do more work than is justified. If an additional capacity gives a species additional inherent worth, why doesn't the greater degree of that capacity give an individual greater worth than others with less of it? Furthermore, why can't a large amount (say 10 units) of one capacity equal a small amount of that capacity (5 units) plus a small amount of another capacity (5 units)? A dog's superior ability to smell might equal our weak capacity to smell plus our weak capacity for taste. An eagle's capacity for sight and flight may equal or exceed our capacity for deliberation. If rationality is inherently worthy, why doesn't possessing more of it grant an individual more inherent value than possessing less of it? Lombardi needs to explain why it is that only kinds (rather than degrees of a kind) count. Until he does so, we may well doubt his conclusion.

Second, premise 3 needs a defense. Doesn't Lombardi commit the naturalistic fallacy in moving from a natural capacity to an inherent value? Speed, beauty, pleasure, knowledge, literacy, practical rationality, and the ability to smell or see may be functionally valuable to different individuals, but functional value is only an instrumental value, not an inherent value. By virtue of what criterion do we decide which capacities are not merely functional but inherently valuable to the degree that their possession gives individuals inherent value? Until split level theorists like Lombardi set forth their grounds for inherent value, their theory must remain merely an interesting hypothesis.

Radical Egalitarianism: The Equal Status Thesis

The codirector of the animal rights group People for the Ethical Treatment of Animals (PETA) has said, "There is no rational basis for separating out the human animal. A rat is a pig is a dog is a boy. They're all mammals. . . . In time, we'll look on those who work in [animal laboratories] with the horror now reserved for the men and women who experimented on Jews in Auschwitz. . . . That, too, the Nazis said, was 'for the greater benefit of the master race.' "[21]

We call the view that equates human beings with animals the equal status thesis. Its foremost proponent is the philosopher Tom Regan, who seeks to achieve three goals related to the treatment of animals: (1) the total abolition of the use of animals in science; (2) the total dissolution of commercial animal agriculture; and (3) the total elimination of commercial and sport hunting and trapping. Even though Regan concedes that some individual uses of animals for biomedical experimentation might be justified and that free-range grazing farming is better than factory farming, all of these uses constitute infringements on animal rights, and the exceptional cases are so isolated as to serve only to confuse the issue.

According to Regan, what is wrong is not the pain caused, the suffering, or the deprivation, though these compound the wrong. What is fundamentally wrong is "the system that allows us to view animals as *our resources*, here for us—to be eaten, or surgically manipulated, or put in our cross hairs for sport or money."[22] Why is it wrong to treat animals as our resources? Because they have inherent value and are ends in themselves just like ourselves. They are of equal worth to human beings.

To say we have equal inherent value is to say that we are something more than, something different from, mere receptacles. Moreover, to insure that we do not pave the way for such injustices as slavery or sexual discrimination, we must believe that all who have inherent value have it equally, regardless of their sex, race, religion, birthplace, and so on. Similarly to be discarded as irrelevant are one's talents or skills, intelligence and wealth, personality or pathology, whether one is loved or admired—or despised and loathed. The genius and the retarded child, the prince and the pauper, the brain surgeon and the fruit vendor, and Mother Theresa and the most unscrupulous used car salesman all have inherent value, all possess it equally, and all have an equal right to be treated with respect, to be treated in ways that do not reduce them to the status of things, as if they exist as resources for others.[23]

What is the basis of the equal inherent value? Just that: "we are each of us the experiencing subject of a life, each of us a conscious creature having an individual welfare that has importance to us whatever our usefulness to others. We want and prefer things; believe and feel things; recall and expect things."[24]

Regan's deontological egalitarianism (rights and respect) argument can be stated thus:

    1. All humans (or all subject-of-a-life humans) have equal positive value.

2. There is no morally relevant difference between humans and (some) animals (for example, mammals).

3. Therefore, all (some) animals have equal positive worth with humans.

4. Moral rights derive from the possession of value.

5. Since humans have rights (to life, not to be harmed, and so on), animals have these same rights.

Several problems arise in Regan's theory of equal inherent value. First, he has not explained why being an experiencing subject entails possessing inherent value. How do we know that being "subject-of-a-life" grants one such inalienable positive value? Is it supposed to be intuitively self-evident? If so, then it would also seem self-evident to some that merely being conscious entails less value than being *self-conscious*, especially *rationally* self-conscious. Someone in a daze or dream may be minimally conscious, but that is a state less valuable than being fully self-conscious with plans and projects. It is desirable to have more reason or intelligence rather than less reason or intelligence. Intelligence, knowledge, and freedom are inherent values, but animals have less of them than humans. It is true that humans have varying degrees of them, but as a species (or on average) we have more of what makes for worth than other species, so that there would seem to be degrees of value among species and within species. If so, we must feel dissatisfied with Regan's assessment. He simply has not given any evidence for the thesis that all animals have equal worth and are to be treated with equal respect.

Regan rejects the notion of differing degrees of inherent value based on differing degrees of self-awareness or some other mental capability, affirming that this leads to the view that mentally superior people have stronger moral rights than mentally inferior people. There are at least two ways to respond to Regan here. First, following deontologists like Kant and Rawls, some may appeal to the threshold view of self-consciousness and argue that all, and only, those who are capable of rational deliberation and life plans are to be accorded a serious right to life. While there may be differences between humans with regard to the ability to reason, almost all (excepting infants, the mentally ill, the senile, the seriously retarded, and the brain damaged) have sufficient ability to be counted within the circle of full moral citizenry. Some higher animals—such as dolphins, gorillas, and chimpanzees—may also belong to this group. I have argued elsewhere that the threshold argument is arbitrary, ad hoc, and unsound.[25]

The second way to respond to Regan's antihierarchical notion of value is to take a contractarian approach to ethics, arguing that there are no inherent values and that animals are not normally part of the social contract. Since rights derive from contract, animals do not have any rights.[26] Of course, the contractarians may still recommend kindness to creatures outside of the contract, but where human interests are compelling, animals may be sacrificed to those interests in ways that humans may not.

What underlies Regan's egalitarianism is the sanctity of life principle, or rather the sanctity of a subject-of-a-life principle, since he views being subject of a life (that is, having beliefs and desires) as intrinsically valuable. But just as the sanctity of life principle fails to distinguish between lives in terms of quality (the life of a bacteria is equal to that of Mother Theresa), the subject-of-a-life principle does the same within a narrower scope. Whereas the former presupposes an outmoded vitalism, the latter presupposes a deeper metaphysics (than Regan offers).[27] Regan offers no defense of this principle, and he has given us no other reason to accept any of his absolutist goals: the total abolition of the use of animals in scientific experimentation; the total dissolution of commercial animal agriculture; and the total elimination of commercial and sport hunting and trapping. Until Regan gives us reason to accept his sanctity of a subject-of-a-life principle, his arguments will fail to support any of these aims.

There is one further problem with Regan's approach that should be mentioned. It fails to explain why we should not intervene in the animal world, eliminating animal cruelty. Shouldn't radical zoophiles go into the wild and protect helpless rabbits, deer, and birds from marauding predators, members of the cat family (lions, tigers, leopards), wolves, and other carnivores? Perhaps carnivores could be confined to separate quarters and fed the carcasses of other animals, including human beings. How can these animal egalitarians rest until all of nature is turned into the peaceable kingdom, where the lion is made to lie down with the lamb? The suffering that wolves cause rabbits or that leopards and tigers cause antelope and deer is far more devastating than what the clean shot of an expert hunter's rifle inflicts.

Both Regan and Paul Taylor (see the next section of this chapter) have difficulty with the violent behavior of wild animals. It does not fit their vision of a peaceable kingdom, but they cannot say that we have duties to eliminate all predatory behavior, let alone all carnivores, to make the world safe for pacifist herbivores and plants, for carnivores cannot help their need for meat. Their "respect for nature" does not allow humans to intervene as environmental imperialists. So what are we to say about the rights of sheep and rabbits not to be torn asunder and harmed by wolves and other predatory animals? Here is Regan's reply. Even though the sheep and rabbits have a right to life and a right not to be harmed, the wolf has no duty to respect those rights, since *ought* implies *can* and the wolf is only doing what is natural and cannot do otherwise. If we intervene we are violating the wolf's right to dinner. Here is Regan's argument.

> [I have] defended [the thesis] that moral patients have *no* duties and thus do not have the particular duty to respect the rights of others. *Only moral agents can have duties,* and this because only these individuals have the cognitive and other abilities necessary for being held morally accountable for what they do or fail to do. Wolves are not moral agents. They cannot bring impartial reason to bear on their decision making—cannot, that is, apply the formal principle of justice or any of its normative interpretations. That being so, wolves in particular and moral patients generally cannot *themselves* meaningfully be said to have duties to anyone, nor, therefore, the particular duty to respect the rights possessed by

other animals. In claiming that we have a *prima facie* duty to assist those animals *whose rights are violated*, therefore, we are not claiming that we have a duty to assist the sheep against the attack of the wolf, since the wolf neither can nor does violate anyone's rights. The absurd results leveled against the attribution of rights to animals simply do not materialize.[28]

I think that Regan is wrong here. If the sheep has a positive right to live in peace, then we have a duty to try to help it. If a boulder came hurling down and was about to crush the sheep, wouldn't we be remiss in our duty if we did not take reasonable steps to get the sheep out of harm's way? Likewise, even if the wolf's actions are natural, we have a duty to the sheep to save it from the wolf.

Furthermore, can't Regan's argument be used to prohibit us from saving humans from wild animals, from bacteria, from insane humans who are only following their nature in raping and killing? Consider the policeman coming to the distraught parents of a child who has been brutally raped and killed by a homicidal maniac. "Well, I would have intervened when I saw Mr. Smith brutalizing your daughter, Mrs. Brown, but then I realized that he was only following his nature as a violent animal, so I was obliged to leave him alone." Or to paraphrase Regan, "You see, Mrs. Brown, in claiming that we have a *prima facie* duty to assist those children *whose rights are violated*, we are not claiming that we have a duty to assist the child against the attack of the madman, since the madman neither can nor does violate anyone's rights." One should note that Regan is inconsistent, for (only eleven pages after saying that we may not intervene in favor of the sheep) he argues that we may kill a rabid dog when it attacks a human.[29] How is this different from when a rabid wolf or dog attacks a sheep?

In the end Regan has not justified either his position or the implications of that position. He holds a deep intuition that all people are of equal worth and appeals to a philosophical consensus on that assumption, which provides a basis for his entire moral theory. From there he argues that since there is no relevant difference between humans and mammals (over the age of one), we should treat all such mammals equally, as possessing equal worth. But if there is no reason to believe that all people, let alone all mammals over the age of one, possess equal positive value, Regan's moral system breaks down and leaves us with no morality at all. We are left with moral nihilism.

Super-Egalitarianism: Biocentric Ethics

> A thing is right when it tends to preserve the integrity, stability, and beauty of the biotic community. It is wrong when it tends otherwise.
>
> —Aldo Leopold, *Sand County Almanac*

One way to approach animal rights is to break our hold on anthropocentrism altogether and view all of life from a perspective of species impartiality. In this regard, one of the most intriguing hypotheses to be put forth in recent years is the Gaia hypothesis of James Lovelock, which views the biosphere as a grand macroorganism, whose several parts interrelate and respond to each other as do the various cells and organs of the body. "Living matter, the air, the oceans, the land surfaces are parts of a giant system . . . [exhibiting] the behavior of a single organism, even a living creature."[30] Gaia is the name of the Greek goddess of earth. According to this view, Gaia has become self-conscious in humanity, and humanity functions as the central nervous system to help protect her from catastrophe. Humanity can harm Gaia by overpolluting and destroying ecosystems, but ultimately Gaia can and will get along without humans. Adopting a Gaian ethic would mean that we seek to promote global or biocentric flourishing. It would constitute a gestalt switch from anthropocentric to biocentric thinking.

Humanists may protest that humans are on average far superior to animals, for we are rational. We can use deductive, abductive, and inductive reasoning in ways that animals cannot. True enough. We do have the virtue, but the question is, why should that virtue count more than the virtues of various animals? The eagle values its visual acuity and its ability to soar through the air more than it does human rationality. The leopard values its fiery speed and ability to leap over bushes and branches in the hunt and scorns our need for weapons with which to kill game. We cannot match the monkey's dexterity, swinging gymnastically from branch to branch, or the squirrel's tightrope walking ability, or the graceful play of the shark cutting a smooth knifelike path through the sea. We cannot digest grass or produce the quantity of milk that a cow gives; we cannot use ultrasonic waves like a bat to get around in the dark. The spider seems to enjoy spinning fine, complex webs that are beyond our power, and if genetic reproduction is the benchmark of evolutionary success, the cockroach has us beat hands down. Stumbling, bumbling, clumsy, landlubbers are we, whose main talent seems to be destroying the ecosystem, threatening animals, and self-servingly prizing ourselves as superior to all others. *Homo sapiens*, "the wise ones," we label ourselves—no other creature approaches our arrogance.

If we take such an impartial, Gaian view of the matter, wouldn't we be forced to give up our anthropocentric bias and take on a more biocentric appreciation of the matter? Rather than overvaluing reason, we would see that it has a special role to play but that other virtues are equally important in the "global scheme of things." All of life is valuable, equally valuable. The new vision is one of biocentric egalitarianism in which humanity occupies but one niche among many important niches, where rather than the conqueror, humanity becomes a steward and plain citizen on a par with other life forms.

But, of course, animals are not normally considered as moral agents. They are moral *patients*, worthy of consideration, but they do not deliberate on right or wrong, do not make moral judgments; so they are not morally responsible for their behavior. A mountain lion who tears up a sheep or deer for dinner or a wolf who ravishes a rabbit is not a bad animal. They are just following their nature, doing what comes naturally, as it were. They cannot act morally or immorally, cannot be praised or blamed, but are innocent. But as living beings, who can be helped or harmed, they are worthy of our moral consideration. They have a right to be left alone, not interfered with, and possibly they should be helped to avoid suffering. To deny that animals (mammals at least) have rights (or are considerable) on the basis of not being rational would force us to deny that small children, the senile, and retarded humans have rights or are morally considerable, since they are relevantly similar to animals in this regard.

While in some ways different from the Gaian hypothesis, especially in that it focuses on individuals rather than on wholes, Paul Taylor's theory of "respect for nature," is the most sustained defense of the biocentric approach to ethics.[31] Taylor sets forth four considerations that together constitute a coherent picture of a species-impartial vision of the value of life. These considerations take on the form of a cumulative argument for biocentric egalitarianism.

1. Humans are not conquerors but simply plain citizens of the earth's community. Their membership is evolutionarily on the same basis as all the nonhuman members.

2. The earth's ecosystem is a complex web of interconnected elements, each sound, functioning element being mutually dependent on the rest.

3. Each individual organism is conceived of as a teleological center of life, pursuing its own good in its own way. Each living being has a particular role to play within a particular niche of the ecosystem, so that each may flourish in its own particular way.

4. Whether we are concerned with standards of merit or with the concept of inherent worth, the claim that humans by their very nature are superior to other species is a groundless claim and, in the light of premises 1–3, must be rejected as nothing more than an irrational bias in our own favor.

5. Therefore, all life forms are of equal inherent positive worth. The good of every individual organism has equal worth and deserves our equal moral consideration.

A brief explication of these premises is in order. I take premise 1 to mean that from the perspective of nature, humans are just one more result of the evolutionary process, no more important than any other aspect of nature.

Premise 2 states a well-known ecological principle that

everything is connected to everything else, so that we never just do one thing. Our actions have wide-ranging implications.

I take premise 3 to mean that each entity in nature has a good and seeks to fulfill its potential. Flowers grow upward toward the light, bees are drawn toward the sustenance of flowers, lions prefer the broad expanse of the wilderness to captivities in zoos, and birds fulfill themselves by soaring upward in the sky and eschewing cages.

Premise 4 is more controversial, but Taylor argues that there is no nonspeciesist way to rank human capacities above animal capacities.

> Such uniquely human characteristics as rationality, aesthetic creativity, individual autonomy, and free will, it might be held, are more valuable than any of the capacities of animals and plants. Yet we must ask: Valuable to whom and for what reason?
>
> The human characteristics mentioned are all valuable to humans. . . . [I]t is from the human standpoint that they are being judged as desirable and good. Humans are claiming superiority over nonhumans from a strictly human point of view, that is, a point of view in which the good of humans is taken as the standard of judgment. All we need to do is to look at the capacities of animals and plants from the standpoint of their good to find a contrary judgment of superiority.[32]

As Taylor recognizes, this is not a valid argument as it stands, for nothing has been said about positive value in the first four premises. So Taylor needs an additional premise. What he offers in premise 5 is something like, "every living thing that has a good is valuable." Living things have interests. It is in the interest of the flower to flourish, in the interest of a tree to grow tall and spread its branches into the sky, in the interest of an eagle to soar gracefully in the heavens, in the interest of a pig to eat in peace, being left alone by humans, and in the interest of humans to live healthy, cooperative, nonviolent, educated lives. We each and all thrive in our own particular way. All living things who have interests, are inherently good.

Even granting Taylor his five principles, I think that the argument commits the naturalist fallacy. It is true that every-thing has a good, a way of flourishing (maybe many ways), but that says nothing about the value of the thing itself. *Having* a good and *being* good, or possessing inherent value, are separate concepts, and the inference from one to the other needs justification. Satan may have a good without being good. Ivan the assassin is good at assassinating czars and commissars, but that does not give him any worth. Likewise, someone may be a good thief, and have a good (that is, be successful) as a thief, without being good. And a properly functioning human immune deficiency virus (HIV) lodged snugly in a cell is flourishing, but I see no reason to say it has inherent worth.

Being good or having inherent value seems relative to having an interest. Consider the concept of good weather. Whether weather is good depends on whose interests are being considered. With regard to the farmer, rain may constitute good weather, whereas this may be bad weather for the sunbather or baseball player. A snowstorm may be bad weather for a person stranded in a car on an open highway but good weather for the owner of a ski resort.

Indeed, Taylor needs to give us an argument for the view that the concept of inherent objective worth is a coherent concept, let alone whether the concept is instantiated. The natural locus of value seems to be the activity of evaluating, which conscious beings engage in. To say that something is valuable is shorthand for the formula "some conscious agent A wants or commends some entity E relative to some standard S and for some purpose P." So we value speedster Spike, who runs the mile in less than 4 minutes, relative to the standards of humans running the mile in races or in hunting for wild animals. Relative to the speed of a cheetah, leopard, sports car, or light wave, Spike's talents are less impressive.

Could we not one-up Taylor's egalitarianism, which equates our high worth with that of animals and plants? Could we not argue that Taylor is right to say that we all—plants, animals, and humans—are of equal value but are wrong in thinking that we have any positive value at all. We all are value-less, worthless (de trop, as Sartre would say). If so, Taylor's argument for biocentric egalitarianism seems to lead to this nihilistic conclusion.

This leads to a second criticism. If all living beings are of equal worth, humans have no valid grounds for preferring the good, or even the survival, of other humans to that of other living beings. I call this the speciesist critique of anthropo-centrism. Although Taylor allows for reasonable self-defense against threats to one's own life or health, biocentric egalitari-anism would prevent us from intervening on behalf of other human beings in their struggle against wolves, sharks, bacteria, and viruses who are only seeking to realize their own good. If bacteria or a dangerous virus invades my body, I have a right to defend myself, but by what criterion is it permissible for doctors to kill these health- or life-threatening bacteria or vi-ruses? Why prefer a human to an HIV's existence? The AIDS patient himself has a right of self-defense to destroy the HIV, but what grounds are there for third parties, like experimenting scientists or doctors, to take sides and engage in viral destruc-tion? Are our scientists and physicians well-paid hit men and women, hired guns to knock off innocent enemies? On Taylor's logic, the HIV virus occupies a niche in the ecosystem and has a good of its own, and as such it is just as valuable as we are. Even more troubling, if the virus is only innocently threatening our health, say with the flu, Taylor's principle of proportionality (harming in proportion to the harm threatened) would seem to prohibit the use of antibiotics.[33] While Taylor may bite the bullet here and simply insist that morality sometimes calls on us to make great sacrifices, most reasonable people will take this implication as a reductio ad absurdum of his egalitarianism. Asking precisely why we reject Taylor's position may help us discover the nature of moral principles.

But I think there is an even more serious problem with Taylor's egalitarianism, one that drives it even further toward nihilism. If racism, sexism, and speciesism are unjustified, discriminatory prejudices, isn't biocentrism also a prejudice? Isn't it biocentric chauvinism? Why ascribe value only to living things and not to nonliving things like robots, computers, cars, mountains, missiles, watches, rocks, air, helium atoms, and dorm rooms? On what basis can we say that an amoeba, but not a robot, has a telos, a good? What is this mysterious substance that gives all, and only, living things inherent worth? Watches have as much telic properties as protozoa, it would seem, and thermostats and self-correcting missiles are as self-regulating as plants.

If living things are completely made from chemicals, aren't these chemicals the true possessors of inherent worth? But the chemicals are composed of atoms, and the atoms of electrons, protons, and neutrons—aren't these then the ultimate centers of value? Living entities are systems, but there are other nonliving systems that can prosper, that have a "good." Dorm rooms and houses can flourish and run down just like living entities. Why is it not immoral to interfere with the flourishing of a dorm room or to smash a rock or destroy a computer or robot as it is to kill an amoeba or fruit fly or cockroach who lives in the dorm room? But if the idea of a good or inherent worth can be extended to things as small as atoms and as complicated as systems and artifacts, how shall we make moral distinctions? Are two rats not worth more than one baby? Two termites more than one house? Two molecules more than one human? The expanding circle of moral considerability expands until nothing is left outside it, and so it ends up as an undifferentiated pantheism beyond good and evil. To make everything equally valuable is to end up without the kind of action-guiding directives that the notion of inherent worth was supposed to provide. It becomes nihilism.

Regan and Taylor seem to hold a Moorean version of the *Good*. For Moore "good" refers to an unanalyzable, simple property like the color yellow, only, unlike yellow, it is nonnatural. It is not empirically identifiable but known through the intuitions. Moore asks us to "imagine one world exceedingly beautiful. Imagine it as beautiful as you can . . . and then imagine the ugliest world you can possibly conceive. Imagine it simply one heap of filth."[34] Even if there were no conscious beings who might derive pleasure or pain in either world, Moore avers, the beautiful one should exist. It would be a good thing for it to exist and a bad thing for the ugly one to exist. For Taylor, apparently, it would be better for trees to exist in peace than for both humans and trees to exist if humans unjustly went about cutting down trees, say, for the purposes of making paper for books—even books about environmental ethics.

Taylor goes so far as to advocate reparations for offended species. We must atone for our former crimes and give special treatment to wetlands and wildflowers. But how do we pay back the bees for all the honey we have stolen from them or the salmon for all the fish we have eaten or all the flukes of roundworms or viruses we have annihilated—we genocidal monsters! What infinite compensation do we owe nature? How can we possibly repay the termites that we have exterminated in favor of our lifeless property?

In the end Taylor's position equates to a moral misanthropy. Killing a wildflower is tantamount to killing a human and may be worse.[35] Since humans are *the* conscious perpetrators of antibiocentric behavior, their demise would not be a bad thing. Note similar sentiments in Edward Abbey's *Desert Solitaire*, where he says that he would sooner shoot a man than a snake.[36] Note Aldo Leopold's famous dictum "A thing is right when it tends to preserve the integrity, stability, and beauty of the biotic community. It is wrong when it tends otherwise."[37] It would follow that if the destruction of the human race would promote the integrity, stability, and beauty of the biotic community, human genocide would be justified. Taylor develops his thesis in great detail. It goes as follows: The well-being of humans is dependent on the well-being of the biosphere (or ecosystem) rather than vice versa. From the point of view of the ecosystem, humans are unnecessary, gratuitous, spongers, parasites.

Every last man, woman, and child could disappear from the face of the earth without any significant detrimental consequence for the good of wild animals and plants. On the contrary, many of them would be greatly benefited. The destruction of their habitats by human "developments" would cease. The poisoning and polluting of their environment would come to an end. The earth's land, air, and water would no longer be subject to the degradation they are now undergoing as the result of large-scale technology and uncontrolled population growth. Life communities in natural ecosystems would gradually return to their former healthy state. Tropical forests, for example, would again be able to make their full contribution to a life-sustaining atmosphere for the whole planet. The rivers, lakes, and oceans of the world would (perhaps) eventually become clean again. Spilled oil, plastic trash, and even radioactive waste might finally, after many centuries, cease doing their terrible work. Ecosystems would return to their proper balance, suffering only the disruptions of natural events, such as volcanic eruptions and glaciation. From these the community of life could recover, as it has so often done in the past. But the ecological disasters now perpetrated on it by humans—disasters from which it might never recover—it would no longer have to endure.[38] The conclusion seems to be: annihilate humanity for the good of the ecosystem!

Animal Rights and the Death of Egalitarianism

Up until now most moral theories ranging from mainline Christian theological ethics to secular deontological and utilitarian ethics have been egalitarian. Each person has equal and positive value, dignity, inviolability. The animal rights advocates, the biocentrist egalitarians, and the like have been successful in forcing us to see that egalitarian ethics has no stopping point. Once we grant the premises that all humans are of equal positive worth and that, qua evolutionarily generated animals ourselves, there is no morally significant difference between human animals and nonhuman animals, we are forced into biocentric egalitarianism, wherein all things have equal worth and have equal moral rights. On the positive side, this view may be a useful myth, prompting us to realize our mutual dependence on nature and leading to beneficial environmental policies. Perhaps humankind lives by myth.

If the biocentrists have won the battle, they have lost the war. Given the secular nature of their enterprise, they have forgotten the historical grounds for attributing to humans positive worth and dignity in the first place, namely, the belief that each of us is created in the image of God, with a mysterious, eternal soul of eternal value. In religion a deep metaphysics grounds the notion of equal human worth and separates us from the rest of nature—we are "a little lower than God," lesser gods. That might not have been good for the rest of the biocentric community, but it did wonders for our self-esteem. But having rejected all deeper metaphysical posits, the secularist wants his cake and wants to eat it too. He wants the fruits of religion without the tree from whence it came. Tolstoy put the point this way: "The attempts to found a morality apart from religion are like the attempts of children who, wishing to transplant a flower that pleases them, pluck it from the roots that seem to them unpleasing and superfluous, and stick it rootless into the ground. Without religion there can be no real, sincere morality, just as without roots there can be no real flower."[39]

Secular egalitarianism leads to animal egalitarianism, which in turn leads to biocentric egalitarianism, which leads to object egalitarianism, which reduces to an absurdity, egalitarian nihilism, wherein no one has value. If everything is equal, then there are no relevant moral distinctions. We are all equal, equally worthless. From the point of view of the universe, we are superfluous. As Hume put it, "The life of a man is of no greater importance to the universe than an oyster."

Is Tolstoy right, then? Is the death of God the death of ethics? Is *secular ethics* an oxymoron? I do not think so. It is just that secular ethics to be credible must be very different from egalitarian ethics. The animal rights debate forces us back to square one, forces us to ask what the point of ethics is in the first place. What is the warrant of practices like rule following, the institution of duties and rights? Well, perhaps there is not just one answer to that question. Perhaps there are many, but one significant point has to do with the resolution of conflicts of interests in a way that staves off a Hobbesian state of nature. Morality seeks to answer the question, How do we best protect our interests and at the same time make the necessary moves to prevent a war of all against all where none of our interests can be realized?

Recall that this is Glaucon's suggestion regarding the origin of justice in the second book of the *Republic*.

> People say that to do wrong is naturally good, to be wronged is bad, but the suffering of injury so far exceeds in badness the good of inflicting it that when men have done wrong to each other and suffered it, and have had a taste of both, those who are unable to avoid the latter and practice the former decide that it is profitable to come to an agreement with each other neither to inflict injury nor to suffer it. As a result they begin to make laws and covenants, and the law's command they call lawful and just. This, they say, is the origin and essence of justice; it stands between the best and the worst, the best being to do wrong without paying the penalty and the worst to be wronged without the power of revenge. The just then is a mean between two extremes; it is welcomed and honored because of men's lack of the power to do wrong.[40]

Socrates rejects such self-interested contractarianism and thus began a search for an ideal, absolutist morality, one that was merged with a Christian metaphysics and led to contemporary egalitarianism. But there is something in Glaucon's description of morality. In fact, it seems most suitable to those of us who have accepted the evolutionary view of human nature.

A possible starting place for resurrecting the ancient compromise contractarian view of ethics is with the new field of sociobiology, which posits the theory that social structures and behavioral patterns, including morality, have a biological base, explained by evolutionary theory. In the past, linking ethics to evolution meant justifying exploitation. Social Darwinism justified imperialism and the principle that might makes right by saying that the law of nature is the survival of the fittest. This philosophy lent itself to a promotion of ruthless egoism. This is nature's law, "nature red in tooth and claw." Against this view, ethologists like Robert Ardrey and Konrad Lorenz argued for a more benign view of the animal kingdom—reminiscent of Rudyard Kipling, where the animal kingdom survives by cooperation, which is at least as important as competition. On Ardrey and Lorenz's view, it is the group or species, not the individual, that is of primary importance.

With the onset of sociobiology in the work of E. O. Wilson and particularly with the work of Robert Trivers, J. Maynard Smith, and Richard Dawkins, a theory has come to the fore that combines radical individualism with limited altruism. It is not the group or species that is of evolutionary importance but the gene, or, more precisely, the gene-type. Genes, the parts of the chromosomes that carry the blueprints for all our natural traits (for example, our height, hair color, skin color, and intelligence), copy themselves as they divide and multiply. At conception they combine with the genes of the member of the opposite sex to form a new individual.

In his fascinating sociobiological study *The Selfish Gene*,[41] Richard Dawkins describes human behavior as determined evolutionarily by stable strategies set to replicate the gene. This is not done consciously, of course, but it is the invisible hand that drives the consciousness. We are essentially gene machines.

Morality—or successful morality—can be seen as an evolutionary strategy for gene replication. Here is an example. Birds are afflicted with life-endangering parasites. Because they cannot use limbs to pick them off their heads, the birds—like much of the animal world—depend on the ritual of mutual grooming. It turns out that nature has evolved two basic types of birds in this regard: those who are disposed to groom anyone (the nonprejudiced type?) and those who refuse to groom anyone but who present themselves for grooming. Dawkins calls the former type of bird "Suckers" and the latter "Cheaters."

In a geographical area with harmful parasites where there are only Suckers or Cheaters, Suckers will do fairly well, but Cheaters will not survive for want of cooperation. But in a Sucker population where a mutant Cheater arises, the Cheater will prosper, and his gene-type will multiply. As the Suckers are exploited, they will gradually die out. But if and when they become too few to groom the Cheaters, the Cheaters will start to die off too and eventually become extinct.

Why don't birds all die off, then? Well, somehow nature has come up with a third type, called "Reciprocators." Reciprocators groom all and only those who reciprocate in the grooming practice. They groom each other and Suckers but not Cheaters. In fact, once a Cheater is caught, he is marked forever. There is no forgiveness. It turns out then that unless there are a lot of Suckers around, Cheaters have a hard time of it—harder even than Suckers! But it is the Reciprocators that prosper. Unlike Suckers they do not waste their time messing with unappreciative Cheaters, so they are not exploited, and they have ample energy to gather food and build better nests for their loved ones.

J. L. Mackie argues that the real name for Suckers is "Christian," but one could say that it applies to all egalitarian forms that promote self-sacrifice or equal rights to animals and other life forms. Cheaters are ruthless egoists who can only survive if there are enough naive Christian-types around. While Reciprocators are reciprocal altruists who have a rational morality based on cooperative self-interest, Suckers like Socrates and Jesus advocate "turning the other cheek and repaying evil with good."[42] Instead of a rule of reciprocity, "I will scratch your back if you will scratch mine," the extreme altruist substitutes the Golden Rule, "If you would like the other fellow to scratch your back, you scratch his—even if he will not reciprocate."

The moral of the story is this: Christian morality (so interpreted) is only rational given the payoff of eternal life (with a scorekeeper—as Woody Allen says in *Crimes and Misdemeanors*). Take that away and it looks like a Sucker-system. What replaces the Christian vision of saintliness is the reciprocal altruist with his tit-for-tat morality, one who is willing to share with those willing to cooperate.

While Mackie may caricature the position of the religious altruist, missing the subtleties of wisdom involved (Jesus said, "Be as wise as serpents but as harmless as doves"),[43] he does remind us that there is a difference between core morality and complete altruism. We have duties to cooperate and reciprocate, but no duty to serve those who manipulate us and no obvious duty to sacrifice ourselves for people outside our domain of special responsibility. We have a special duty of high altruism toward those in the close circle of our concern, namely, our family and friends.

Secular egalitarianism leads to animal egalitarianism, which leads to biocentric egalitarianism, which leads to egalitarian nihilism. What the animal rights advocates have forced us to see is that egalitarianism is dead. What postegalitarian moral philosophers must do is rebuild a nonegalitarian ethics based not on the inviolability of humanity or on animal needs or on life but on reciprocity and merit. True enough, it will be not a pre-egalitarian but a postegalitarian ethic; for we have learned a great deal from the egalitarians, namely, that the range of moral considerability was too narrow, that skin color and gender and even species membership are not morally relevant criteria. Like the bird Reciprocators, we are willing to cooperate with the rest for the good of all.[44] It will be a world of equal opportunity but not reverse discrimination.

If my argument is correct, the minimal status view on animal rights turns out to be the correct moral position. Animals are not to be given rights that proceed from the moral contract, but they are to be treated kindly (or noncruelly). Refraining from unnecessary harm would doubtless cause us to transform our agricultural industry, eliminating animal factories, but it is unlikely it would lead to a moratorium on animal research for scientific purposes.

The Egalitarian Objection to Contractarian Inegalitarianism

Finally, I should respond to the major criticism of inegalitarian ethics. Regan sets forth the criticism in an attack on perfectionism, those ethical systems that grade people according to some criterion like reason or intelligence or ability to deliberate. Regan never argues for egalitarianism directly, but he argues that all the alternatives are counterintuitive, especially perfectionism, and that egalitarianism is the only possible choice. Here is his entire argument against inegalitarian perfectionism.

> Perfectionist theories of justice are morally pernicious, providing as they do, the foundation of the most objectionable forms of social, political, and legal discrimination—chattel slavery, rigid caste systems, and gross disparities in the quality of life available to citizens in the same state, for example. But perfectionist theories are objectionable at a deeper level. Whether individuals have the talent necessary to acquire the favored virtues (e.g., ability to do higher mathematics) is beyond their control. What natural talents individuals have, to [rely on] . . . a helpful phrase of Rawls's, is the result of "the natural lottery." Those who are born with intellectual or artistic gifts have not themselves done anything to deserve preferred treatment, any more than those who are born lacking these gifts have done anything to deserve being denied those benefits essential to their welfare. No theory of justice can be adequate that builds justice on so fortuitous a foundation, one that could sanction forwarding the "higher" interests of some over the vital interests of others, even to the point where the latter could be enslaved by the former, thereby having their liberty and other benefits acutely diminished, *in the name of justice*. Though consensus is a rare thing in the cloakrooms of philosophy, few, if any, philosophers today would defend a perfectionist theory of justice, for the reasons given.[45]

I think that this passage contains a bundle of confusions. First of all, it is not clear exactly what features of existence are not part of "the natural lottery." True enough our genetic endowment is something that we have not earned. What follows from that? That what we do with our natural endowment is not ours to keep? But if everything we have, including our virtues, industry, effort, and hard work, are to be discounted as granting us ownership or desert, then even our "moral acts" are undeserved, and we do not deserve praise for them or censure for our viciousness. Then nothing counts, and it really does not matter what we do, does it?

But this is the wrong way of looking at the matter. Just as being born a human with a rich genetic endowment distinguishes us from termites and cockroaches as far as abilities and life chances are concerned, so those with richer genetic and environmental endowments will have better abilities and life chances than those with less favored conditions. Suppose I agree that a criminal who is going to try to rob, rape, and kill my friends and me had a bad shake by the natural lottery. So what? So have rabid dogs and cockroaches and termites. I am still going to protect myself from the criminal and them. Our genetic endowments and early environmental conditioning define who we are, and to attempt to sweep away these distinctions because we did not earn them is to misunderstand what personal identity and responsibility are all about.

Regan uses the bogeymen of slavery and caste systems to frighten us into egalitarianism. Perfectionist theories of justice are "morally pernicious, providing as they do, the foundation of . . . chattel slavery, rigid caste systems, and gross disparities." The perfectionist may respond in either of two ways. First, the perfectionist may argue that so long as stupid people or animals are treated kindly, there is nothing inherently wrong with slavery or at least nothing absolutely wrong with it. The wrongness of slavery consists in subordinating *autonomous* beings unjustly or treating humans and animals cruelly, but if some humans or animals are not capable of significant autonomy, what is wrong with paternalistic ownership? Second, the perfectionist may agree that slavery does not follow from its premises, for the perfectionist may well be committed to promoting maximal freedom. Since slavery violates freedom, a perfectionist would be inclined to take a strong moral stand against the practice even apart from egalitarian principles.

Finally, Regan's point about egalitarianism being a consensus postulate among philosophers only shows how much "politically correct" thinking has invaded the halls of wisdom. I think that Regan is correct. Egalitarianism is accepted by almost every ethicist today. What I have tried to show in this chapter is that considering the problem of animal rights shows us that egalitarianism leads to absurdities and should be rejected for a more rational ethical theory, one close to what Regan dismisses as perfectionism, based on merit and reciprocity, not equal positive worth or dignity—unless, of course, one can find a deeper metaphysical basis for morality.

Notes

John Jagger, John Kleinig, Wallace Matson, Michael Levin, Sterling Harwood, and Paul Taylor made helpful criticisms of a previous draft of this paper, for which I am grateful.

1. I think Regan is correct about the egalitarian consensus. I have examined several versions of contemporary egalitarianism in my paper, "A Critique of Contemporary Egalitarianism," *Faith and Philosophy* 8, no. 4 (October 1991): 481–504. Mary Anne Warren is an example of a moral philosopher who holds to the necessity of egalitarianism: "Any human morality, to be workable in the long run, must recognize the equal moral status of all persons, whether through a postulate of equal basic moral rights or in some other way. The recognition of the moral equality of other persons is the price we must each pay for their recognition of our moral equality. Without this mutual recognition of moral equality, human society can exist only in a state of chronic and bitter conflict" ("Difficulties with the Strong Animal Rights Position," *Between the Species* 2, no. 4 [fall 1987]: 163–73).

2. René Descartes, *Discourse on Method*, in *The Philosophical Works of Descartes*, 2 vols., trans. Elizabeth Haldane and G. R. T. Ross (Cambridge: Cambridge University Press, 1911), vol. 1, pp. 79–130.

3. From Nicholas Fontaine's *Memoirs*, quoted in Peter Singer, *Animal Liberation* (New York: Avon, 1976), p. 220.

4. Both quotations are cited in Cleveland Amory, *Man Kind? Our Incredible War on Wildlife* (New York: Harper & Row, 1974), pp. 219, 244. Richard Garner made me aware of these citations.

5. Cited in M. T. Phillips and J. Sechzer, *Animal Research and Ethical Conflict* (New York: Springer-Verlag, 1989), pp. 75–76.

6. William Whewell, *Lectures*, cited in Peter Singer and Tom Regan, eds., *Animal Rights and Human Obligations*, (Englewood Cliffs, N.J.: Prentice-Hall, 1976) p. 131.

7. Philip Austin, *Our Duty Towards Animals* (London: Kegan Paul, Trench & Co., 1885).

8. Stephen Stitch, "Do Animals Have Beliefs?" *Australasian Journal*

of *Philosophy* 57, no. 1 (March 1979): 15–28; R. G. Frey, *Interests and Rights: The Case Against Animal Rights* (Oxford: Clarendon Press, 1980).

9. Gen. 1:28–29 Revised Standard Version.

10. Thomas Aquinas, *Summa Theologica* (London: Benziger Brothers, 1918), part 2, question 64, article 1.

11. Thomas Aquinas, *Summa Contra Gentiles* (London: Benziger Brothers, 1928), book 3, part 2, chapter 112.

12. Immanuel Kant, *Lectures on Ethics*, trans. Louis Infield (New York: Harper & Row, 1963), p. 239.

13. Jeremy Bentham, *Introduction to Principles of Morals and Legislation* (London: T. Payne, 1789), chapter 17, section 1.

14. Pojman, *Ethics: Discovering Right and Wrong* (Belmont, Calif.: Wadsworth Publishing Co., 1990), chapter 5, pp. 73–89.

15. Peter Singer, *Animal Liberation*, p. 5. Note that Singer interprets *interests* broadly as desires. See Singer, *Practical Ethics* (Cambridge: Cambridge University Press, 1980), p. 12. Singer's *Animal Liberation* is more a manifesto on animal rights than a definitive argument, and as such it has awakened scores of thousands, including myself, to the moral status of animals.

16. Singer, *Animal Liberation*, p. 108.

17. Singer, "Animal Liberation," *New York Review of Books*, April 5, 1973, p. 17.

18. Singer, "Animals and the Value of Life," in *Matters of Life and Death*, ed. Tom Regan (New York: Random House, 1980), p. 236; also in *Animal Liberation*, pp. 21–22. Not all animals are of equal worth. As Singer says,

A rejection of speciesism does not imply that all lives are of equal worth. While self-awareness, intelligence, the capacity of meaningful relations with others, and so on are not relevant to the question of inflicting pain—since pain is pain, whatever other capacities, beyond the capacity to feel pain, the being may have—these capacities may be relevant to the question of taking life. It is not arbitrary to hold that the life of a self-aware being, capable of abstract thought, of planning for the future, of complex acts of communication, and so on, is more valuable than the life of a being without these capacities. To see the difference between the issues of inflicting pain and taking life, consider how we would choose within our own species. If we had to choose to save the life of a normal human or a mentally defective human, we would probably choose to save the life of the normal human; but if we had to choose between preventing pain in the normal human or the mental defective—imagine that both have received painful but superficial injuries, and we only have enough painkiller for one of them—it is not nearly so clear how we ought to choose. The same is true when we consider other species. The evil of pain is, in itself, unaffected by the other characteristics of the being that feels the pain; the value of life is affected by these other characteristics.

19. R. G. Frey, *Rights, Killing, and Suffering* (Oxford: Basil Blackwell, 1983), chapter 4. My discussion of Singer has profited greatly from Frey's book.

20. Martin Benjamin, "Ethics and Animal Consciousness," in *Social Ethics*, eds. Thomas Mappes and Jane Zembaty (Englewood Cliffs, N.J.: Prentice-Hall, 1982), pp. 394–401. Mary Anne Warren, "Difficulties with the Strong Animal Rights Position"; Donald VanDeVeer, "Interspecific Justice," pp. 51–66, in Donald VanDeVeer and Christine Pierce, eds., *People, Penguins, and Plastic Trees* (Belmont, Calif.: Wadsworth Publishing Co., 1986); Louis Lombardi, "Inherent Worth, Respect, and Rights," *Environmental Ethics* 5 (fall 1983): 257–70. Warren's position is that all sentient animals, capable of having experiences, have moral rights, but that the rights are not equal in strength to those of persons.

21. The quotation is attributed to Ingrid Newberg by K. McCabe, "Who Will Live, Who Will Die," *Washingtonian*, August 1986, and "Beyond Cruelty," *Washingtonian*, February 1990.

22. Tom Regan, "The Case for Animal Rights," in *In Defense of Animals*, ed. Peter Singer (Oxford: Basil Blackwell, 1985). In criticizing Regan's position, I should note that I have learned much from him and consider his work of a high caliber.

23. Regan, "Case for Animal Rights."

24. Regan, "Case for Animal Rights."

25. Pojman, "Are Human Rights Based on Equal Human Worth?" forthcoming in *Philosophy and Phenomenological Research*, and "Critique of Contemporary Egalitarianism."

26. Perhaps some animals are part of the social contract. Sterling Harwood suggests that they may be. "I give my dog reasonable expectations. He relies on me and I on him. We have understanding and routines. Both humans and dogs are creatures of habit. And the relations between humans and dogs are quite standardized. . . . There are

any number of statutes on the books specifying our rights and duties concerning animals. That sounds like enough of a social contract" (Letter to author, March 22, 1992).

27. Pojman, *Life and Death: Grappling with the Moral Dilemmas of Our Time* (Boston: Jones & Bartlett, 1992), chapter 2.

28. Regan, *The Case for Animal Rights* (Berkeley, Calif.: University of California Press, 1983), pp. 284–85. Paul Taylor argues in a similar vein that we may not interfere with animals and kill natural predators of a species, such as the wolf attacking a deer. Why should we support noninterference for wolves but not for wolflike men? See Taylor, *Respect for Nature* (Princeton, N.J.: Princeton University Press, 1986), p. 195.

29. Regan, *Case for Animal Rights*, p. 296.

30. James Lovelock and Sidney Epton, "The Quest of Gaia," *New Scientist* 65 (February 6, 1975): 305. I am indebted to John Kleinig's discussion in *Valuing Life* (Princeton, N.J.: Princeton University Press, 1991), pp. 73–88, for an understanding of the Gaia hypothesis. I should add that I am skeptical about the Gaian hypothesis. The earth does not exhibit any of the teleonomic traits characteristic of organisms who have purposes or conscious interests. Evolution may mimic purposiveness, but the order of origin is in the opposite direction.

31. Paul Taylor, "The Ethics of Respect for Nature," *Environmental Ethics* 3 (fall 1981): 197–218; reprinted in Donald VanDeVeer and Christine Pierce, eds., *People, Penguins, and Plastic Trees*, 169–84, and in Taylor, *Respect for Nature*. Compared with the biocentric revolutionary Taylor, Singer is a reformist and Regan an animal abolitionist. Singer is soft on carnivores; Regan limits his protection to mammals above the age of one year; but Taylor advocates not only global noninterference but strong affirmative action for termites and wildflowers.

32. Taylor, "Ethics of Respect for Nature," pp. 129–30.

33. Taylor responds to this point:

> Your second criticism is important. . . . The problem is complex, and I am not sure how to solve it. . . . I have yet to see a good argument (that doesn't rely on our intuitive judgments, which are simply embedded in our culture's anthropocentrism), for unequal degrees of "moral significance" attached to different species. What has to be shown, it seems to me, is that the *intrinsic* (inherent) *value* (worth) of organisms varies with what species they belong to. Although this *seems* to be obviously true, the more it is critically examined the more it turns out to be just an assumed belief that is part

of the value-conditioning we all receive from our culture. It has the same status as racial bias in a racist culture, or a sexist bias in our culture! (Letter to author, March 19, 1993)

34. Moore, *Principia Ethica* (Cambridge, Mass.: Cambridge University Press, 1903), p. 83.

35. Taylor, "Ethics of Respect for Nature," p. 130.

36. Edward Abbey, *Desert Solitaire* (New York: Ballantine Books, 1968), p. 20.

37. Aldo Leopold, *Sand County Almanac* (Oxford: Oxford University Press, 1949), pp. 224–25.

38. Paul Taylor, *Respect for Nature*, p. 176. Sally M. Gearhart says, "An extraterrestrial observing our polluted and diseased planet would have to conclude that homo sapiens, the inventor of technology, was an evolutionary blunder and should now silently fold its wings and steal away. I agree with that cosmic observer. From the point of view of our fellow species and the earth itself, the best that can happen is that human beings never conceive another child, that the child being conceived at this very moment be the last human being ever to exist." ("An End to Technology: A Modest Proposal," in *Machina Ex Dea: Feminist Perspectives on Technology*, ed. Joan Rothschild (New York: Pergamon Press, 1983), pp. 171–83. Sterling Harwood pointed this quote out to me.

39. Tolstoy, "Religion and Morality," in *Leo Tolstoy, Selected Essays* (New York: Modern Library, 1964), pp. 7–32.

40. Plato *Republic* 2.358e.

41. Richard Dawkins, *The Selfish Gene* (Oxford: Oxford University Press, 1976), chapter 10.

42. J. L. Mackie, "The Law of the Jungle: Moral Alternatives and Principles of Evolution," *Philosophy* 53 (October 1978): 455–64. Sterling Harwood wrote that Ted Turner said, "Christianity is a religion for losers." (Letter to author, March 22, 1992.)

43. Matt. 10:16 Revised Standard Version.

44. My version of the ethics of reciprocity owes an initial inspiration to Howard Kahane's "Making the World Safe for Reciprocity," in *Reason and Responsibility*, ed. Joel Feinberg, 6th ed. (Belmont, Calif.: Wadsworth Publishing Co., 1985), pp. 495–502. In my version, the ideal of a good will, including a general principle of not being cruel or doing unnecessary harm, plays a necessary role. Contrast this no harm principle with Singer's equal consideration of interest principle. For Singer all animals are equal, so that if a dog and a child are in pain and we have only one pain reliever, we have a moral dilemma, since

their interests are similar. On the no harm principle (*Primum non nocere*), we would unhesitatingly give the pain reliever to the child, since we value humans (persons) more highly than animals. When Singer writes, "What, for instance, are we to do about genuine conflicts of interest like rats biting slum children? I am not sure of the answer," the anthropocentric principle responds with an immediate, "We kill the rats, since children's interests outweigh those of other animals." It is not that animals lack interests but simply that we have a stronger duty to protect our children.

45. Regan, *Case for Animal Rights*, p. 234.

6

Education for Self-Knowledge and Worthy Living

David L. Norton

Over the past decade, public awareness of serious deficiencies in America's pattern of education has been aroused by a succession of commission reports whose conclusions are epitomized in the famous words of one of them: "If an unfriendly foreign power had attempted to impose on America the mediocre educational performance that exists today, we might well view it as an act of war."[1] The focus of attention has been upon the declining performance of American students at reading, writing, math, and science, relative to students of many other nations as measured by scores on international standardized tests. I think this focus is dangerous in two ways: it diverts attention from deeper deficiencies in our educational pattern, and it generates proposals for reform that will have the effect of increasing the extent to which students are trained for test taking.

The discrepancy between skill at test taking and resourcefulness at dealing with concrete problems of living is largely responsible for what is becoming recognized as an educational crisis in Japan. Japanese students are the world's best test takers, but Japanese employers have begun to complain that their entry-level employees have not learned how to think. As an example of the discrepancy between test-taking ability and real-life performance, all Japanese study English in school for six years, but an American in a Tokyo train station is extremely lucky to find anyone who can give him directions in English. Few Japanese will attempt to converse in English, because their studies of the language were aimed solely at passing written tests.

We are told that to improve the standing of our students on international standardized tests, teaching must be intensified, class work must be made more rigorous, schooldays must be lengthened, vacations must be shortened, and homework must be increased. I think the predictable outcome of these measures will be to multiply the numbers of turned-off, tuned-out students who presently crowd our classrooms at every level, as today Japan faces a mounting "school refuser" situation. To do more of what we are presently doing, and to do it more intensively, presupposes that what we are doing is basically right but we are not doing enough of it. My counterclaim is that what we are doing is fundamentally wrong because it extinguishes in too many children the innate eagerness to learn that characterizes human beings until they encounter classroom force-feeding. Later I am going to add to this the charge that our educational system leaves entirely untouched what should be its central mission. Then I will conclude by connecting these two foundational deficiencies and arguing that their magnitude is such as to dwarf the problem of declining scores on international tests.

Research in educational psychology over the past forty years has demonstrated conclusively that human beings begin life as active learners,[2] and this finding merely confirms what every attentive parent already knew. The infant in its crib can be heard practicing sound formation; the two-year-old takes great delight at each new-found capability and struggles to improve it; the three-year-old longs to be four because of what four-year-olds can do that three-year-olds cannot.

But by the mid-elementary grades, too many children exhibit no love of schooling whatever; and our high schools imprison large numbers of leaden-eyed, resigned, cynical, or actively resistant "learners." From his on-site studies of high schools, Theodore Sizer drew a representative conclusion: "Lamentably, far too few modern American adolescents are hungry students. No more important finding has emerged from . . . our studies than that the American high school student is all too often docile, compliant, and without initiative." And Sizer adds, "Some who have initiative use it to undertake as little engagement as possible with school."[3]

What has happened?

A common hypothesis is that learning loses its delight as it increases in difficulty, or as this is sometimes put, when learning changes from "play" to "work." But an important finding of the research in educational psychology that I referred to a moment ago is that the learning that infants do is the most difficult of all—so difficult that we still cannot understand how they do it. With remarkable insight, Alfred North Whitehead perceived this many years ago, and it led him to attack the conventional ordering of the curriculum according to degrees of difficulty:

> It is not true that the easier subjects should precede the harder. On the contrary, some of the hardest must come first because nature so dictates, and because they are essential to life. The first intellectual task which confronts an infant is the acquirement of spoken language. What an appalling task, the correlation of meanings with sounds! . . . We all know that an infant does it, and that the miracle of his achievement is inexplicable. But so are all miracles, and yet to the wise they remain miracles. All I ask is that with this example staring us in the face we should cease talking nonsense about postponing the harder subjects.[4]

I think we should also cease talking nonsense about the difficulty of a task having the effect of diminishing the pleasure of doing it. The profounder insight is Aristotle's—that the greater the difficulty of the task, the keener the satisfaction in doing it, provided it is the right task for the person who is engaged at it. But the particular nonsense that Aristotle here overturns is, unfortunately, quite dear to twentieth-century American common sense. One day, in conversation with a group of my neighbors, I happened to say that I enjoyed my work. Their collective response was expressed by one of them: "Well, then, it isn't real work."

The issue between Aristotle and American common sense is settled in favor of Aristotle by our children, if we will set aside our preconceptions in order to perceive them accurately. Here is a statement by a good observer, a veteran teacher at an alternative school in Newark, Delaware: "Interesting work over which students are given some significant measure of control elicits great effort."[5] Here are the words of another good observer, the founder of an alternative school called "Children's Village" (Nonami Kodomo-no Mura) in Nagoya, Japan: "I discovered that children have a deep natural desire to learn, and that they will work hard and long if they are permitted to learn what they want to learn in their own way and at their own pace."[6]

Lapse of the love of learning by the mid-elementary grades is perceived, and frequently bemoaned, by our public school-teachers and educators, but most of them profess innocent bewilderment, as if they were confronting an unfortunate law of nature.[7] But the transformation has been produced not by a malevolent law of nature but by bureaucratized, depersonalized, authoritarian public education.

From my observations of elementary school classrooms, it is easy to pinpoint when and how the transformation begins. The assault on children's innate love of learning begins in first grade by ignoring what children spontaneously want to find out about and substituting what the curriculum says they "need" to learn. Typically the curriculum is decided by "experts" who are far removed from children in their classrooms, and teachers have no input.[8] Ultimately the authority of the curriculum designers is their knowledge of the adult life for which children must be prepared, and their justification for ignoring children is that children know nothing of adult life.

But children know what they want to learn about now, and a curriculum that imperiously overrides this severs its connection with children's innate desire to learn and must rely upon manufactured incentives. At a stroke, *learning in order to find out* is expelled from the classroom in favor of learning for grades, credits, honors, and diplomas, together with the social approval that comes with these. From this point on, the educational system requires that children work for extrinsic rewards alone. Given twelve or sixteen years of this kind of conditioning, it is no wonder that Americans are typified by my neighbors who define work in terms of extrinsic rewards exclusively.

I have spoken to the *when* and the *how* of the transformation of learning from its roots in student curiosity to its preoccupation with extrinsic rewards, but it remains to say something about the *why*. In essence, the *why* is answered by the famous motto of Calvin Coolidge, "The business of America is business." Since the Industrial Revolution, the economic success of the West has been based upon the progressive transfer of the control of work from workers themselves to management.[9] This culminated in the first quarter of our century with the "scientific management" of Frederick W. Taylor, which demonstrated that efficiency of production is achieved when management dictates in minute detail how work is to be done and workers strictly obey. The effect, of course, was to eliminate the initiatives of workers in the workplace, and this in turn eradicated their interest in the work. A basic premise of Taylor's was that work is done for money alone.

The *Encyclopedia Britannica* says of Taylor's book *The Principles of Scientific Management* that it "influenced the development of virtually every country enjoying the benefits of modern industry."[10] Taylor contended that the principles of scientific management were applicable to every kind of productive organization, and almost immediately after the book's publication in 1911, the swelling ranks of Taylorites in our country targeted America's schools as examples of gross inefficiency that cried out for scientific management. Over the next decade, scientific management swept through the National Education Association and reshaped our schools. Schools learned unself-consciously to regard themselves as businesses, producing "products" for the "market," and responsible for doing so with maximum efficiency.[11] Almost no one disputed Taylor's contention that maximum efficiency requires total management control. This is the kind of management that prevails in our schools today. Good "classroom management" is total control by teachers of everything that occurs, and good school management is total control of teachers and staff by school administrators. In the name of efficiency, this kind of management serves to eradicate all spontaneous conduct of students, including expression of their spontaneous interests, on the ground that all student initiative that is spontaneous—that is, all initiative that is not the product of classroom conditioning—is disruptive of the educational enterprise.

Ironically, American business and industry are at present desperately attempting to restructure themselves to regain the spontaneous initiatives of workers that were eliminated by command-and-control management. The cornerstone of the restructuring is the replacement of command-and-control management by what is termed facilitative or participative management, under which workers participate in both the design of their work and the management of their companies. Meanwhile, our schools are still grinding out "products" of twelve or sixteen years of conditioning in passive receptivity under command-and-control management in their classrooms.

Students who work for grades alone become employees who work for money alone. And employees who work for money alone have in the end priced American goods out of both foreign and domestic markets. American business and industry are in desperate need of the revival of the intrinsic rewards of work, but our young people have no notion of the intrinsic rewards of work, because their primary work—their studies—has been systematically drained of intrinsic rewards in favor of the extrinsic rewards whose distribution is entirely controlled by teachers and school administrators.

Now I will turn to the college level of American education, where I have been employed for twenty-six years. I find that my undergraduates have predictably little or no idea of intrinsically rewarding work. Regarding their studies, I sometimes find that they can distinguish an occasional course whose work they find satisfying to do in and for itself, but typically they regard this as a happy accident that has no bearing on their choice of their adult course of life.

I say to my students, "There are countless things you can do to earn money in your adult life; why not choose something that you truly like doing?" I say, "There are countless organizations in our society that pay people to do things; why not find what you truly like to do, and then hunt up an organization that will pay you to do it?" The response from most is utter bewilderment, as if I were speaking a foreign language. A few turn wide-eyed and become noticeably energized, but typically this lapses in a day or a week. What they like to do, they tell me, is lie out at the beach, ski, go to rock concerts, hang out with their friends, and buy cars, clothes, stereos, and so on, and no one will pay them to do these things.

Abraham Maslow phoned me one night, during his tenure as chair of the psychology department at Brandeis University, and in an urgent tone put the question, "Where can I get hold of a bunch of little kids?" To my startled return question, "Why, Abe; what's the matter?" he replied morosely, "We get them too late." (I found him a Unitarian Sunday School class.) Abe was right; our college students make vocational choices on the basis of projected material rewards alone, because they are products of twelve years of prior conditioning at working exclusively for extrinsic rewards in their classrooms.

My conclusion is that our entire pattern of education ignores its primary obligation, which is to equip young people for the most important choices human beings ever make. I term these *life-shaping choices*, by which I refer to the commitments that lay down our adult courses of life, fashioning our mature identities and character. They include choice of vocation, choice of whether to marry and whom to marry; choice of whether to have children, how many to have, and when to have them;

choice of avocations; choice of which friendships to cultivate; choice of locale of permanent residence (or vagabondage, where appropriate); and choice of religious and civic commitments. My contention is that our pattern of education does nothing to help young people make sound rather than unsound life-shaping choices. To be sure, our pattern is designed to equip them for the vocations they choose; it is the soundness of the choice itself that is ignored.

There are, I think, three necessary conditions for soundness in regard to life-shaping choices. One of them is the logical condition of sufficient knowledge of alternatives, without which our meaning of the term *choice* cannot apply. Another is the developmental condition of self-knowledge, in the absence of which the choices we make are not in the deepest sense ours. The remaining condition is that each life-shaping choice must complement, and not conflict with, the individual's other life-shaping choices. We can call this the condition of integrity— *integrity* understood here as the harmonious integration of the parts of a whole, the whole in this case being the individual life.

Regarding knowledge of alternatives, there is no way to gain it except by exploration—young people must "try on" many things—but we curb exploration by our institutionalized pattern of education as sixteen-years-at-one-sitting. Adolescence is inherently outfitted for exploration by the adventurousness that marks this stage of life. When Robert Louis Stevenson said, "Youth is wholly experimental,"[12] he was echoing Homer, Aristotle, Shakespeare, and many other keen observers of this stage through the ages. But in our society, adolescent adventurousness is equated with irresponsibility. Instead of recognizing adolescence as a distinctive stage of development with its own inherent developmental requirements, we regard it as a temporary aberration in an otherwise sensible life and believe ourselves to be doing it a service by squeezing it between prolonged expectations of the dependent behavior of childhood and premature expectations of the committed living of adulthood. In the words of sociologist James C. Coleman, our society "has no place for an intermediate status between full dependency, which a person is in when he is in school, and the full productivity that he is in when he is in the labor force."[13]

Accordingly, it is unsurprising that most of my undergraduates have no direct acquaintance with any of the innumerable vocations that are open to their choice—and this includes the vocations that they in fact choose. For the past fifteen years I have asked my students to write for me a page or two on the most interesting job that they have held, and in certain cases I follow this up with an interview. I analyze what they provide on about twenty parameters, and we devote two or three classes to discussion of this. To set down all I have learned from them would require a book, and it includes many admirable things, many touching things, and many humorous things. But here I will focus on just two or three matters that I believe to have crucial implications for worthy living.

Just 8 percent of my students have had occasion to discover the incomparable satisfaction of doing something significant for others. Typically this is by working in a summer camp for handicapped or disadvantaged children or by performing a rescue as a lifeguard. One student spent a summer helping families put their homes together in the aftermath of a flood. Another fought forest fires and on one occasion helped to save a threatened town. Almost uniformly this 8 percent reports being significantly changed by the experience, such that they are resolved never to be without this special satisfaction in later life. But what of the 92 percent that have no such experience? I find that too many of them are convinced egoists, believing that all human beings live to serve their own interests exclusively.

Only 2 percent of my students have ever done work pertaining to their chosen careers—for example, working in a law office when one is planning to become a lawyer—and *half of these* have learned from the experience that their career choice was a mistake. The hazard for the remaining 98 percent is that classroom preparation for an occupation and working at that occupation are often very different in what I will term their *existential tonality*. It is akin to the difference between reading about a place—say Alaska—and living there; and if everyone who fell in love with Alaska by reading about it also loved living there, Alaska would be as populous as India. To the degree that preparation for a vocation and practice of it differ in existential tonality, persons who choose their vocation without hands-on experience of it have little notion of what they are committing themselves to.

Only 1 percent of my students have ever worked at a job that was objectively interesting, which I define as one whose description would be likely to hold the attention of a stranger at a bus stop. Moreover, almost none of them has so much as entertained the aim of seeking a summer job or a job between high school and college that would be inherently interesting to themselves. They take earning money to be the sole reason for working and have no idea that by exercising a little more initiative, they can equip themselves with growth experiences that pay large dividends in terms of the quality of their later lives.

The exploration that is the means for acquiring the knowledge of alternatives that is a logical condition of choice is also the means by which self-knowledge is acquired, but before showing that this is the case, something must be said about the importance of self-knowledge as a necessary condition of sound life-shaping choices. What I will term *philosophies of life* are systems of thought whose focus is the qualitative improvement of human lives. They include prominent forms of Hinduism, Mahayana Buddhism, the eudaimonism of Plato and Aristotle and especially of Socrates, the thought of Emerson and Thoreau, in some measure the pragmatism of James and Dewey, and the resurgence in the past decade of what is termed *virtues ethics*. A distinguishing characteristic of philosophies of life is the priority they give to self-knowledge. They do this on the contention that the paramount question that is posed to every person by the fact of being born a human being is, "What kind of life shall I lead?" This is a question of direction, and it is answered by what I have described as the life-shaping choices, each of which lays a course for the individual into his or her future, and all of which must be integrated into a unified life of a particular kind, thereby manifesting the virtue of integrity.

Self-knowledge is composed of what I will term *personal truths,* and their distinctiveness as a class becomes evident by contrast to the two kinds of truths that have been the focus of modern Western epistemology, namely, "truths of fact," or empirical truths, and "truths of reason," or "rational truths." Examples of empirical truths are "The earth revolves around the sun" and "The color of my desk is brown." Examples of rational truths are "Two plus two is four" and "If A is greater than B, and B is greater than C, then A is greater than C."

It takes but a moment's reflection to recognize that each of us is capable of enunciating thousands of truths of fact and thousands of truths of reason. It is just as notable that nothing in the realms of truths of fact and truths of reason affords to any person the least guidance with respect to the course that his or her life should take. Because this is so, I will term truths of both of these kinds *nondirectional.* By contrast, what I am terming personal truths are directional; they indicate the best course of life for each individual. When Socrates describes himself as philosopher, gadfly, and midwife, he is identifying his course of life. What I have termed philosophies of life hold that there is a distinctive course of life that is right for each individual, amid countless possibilities. This is the individual's vocation, variously termed his or her "genius," "daimon," "Buddha nature," or "atman." It consists in innate potentialities that predispose persons to a particular direction in life. As distinguished from other possibilities, the actualization by an individual of his or her potentialities affords intrinsic rewards to that person—that is, the activity is personally fulfilling and satisfying. Self-knowledge, then, is knowledge of the activities, situations, and relationships that the individual experiences as intrinsically rewarding. Engaged at these, the individual invests the best of himself or herself and strives continuously to improve, while in the process contributing objective values to others.

By ignoring self-knowledge, our pattern of education fails

to equip young people for the life-shaping choices that will form their identities and their character in adult life. This reflects the neglect of personal truths by modern epistemology, and the reason for the neglect is the faulty notion of "objectivity" in the foundations of modern epistemology. In the beginnings of modernity, *objectivity* and *subjectivity* were defined disjunctively— they were thought to exclude one another. It followed from this that the quest for objective truth called upon researchers to extinguish the influence of their own subjectivity—their personal feelings, hopes, fears, and so on. From that time to the present, an interest by individuals in self-knowledge has been subject to the charge of narcissistic self-indulgence.

I have said that exploration is required for self-knowledge. We cannot know what types of conduct, situations, and relationships will afford us intrinsic rewards without experience of varieties of conduct, situations, and relationships. The appropriate place for exploration is adolescence, which by contrast to childhood possesses the measure of autonomy that exploration requires, and which by contrast to adulthood is as yet uncommitted to a chosen course of life. And adolescence is equipped for exploration by its inherent adventurousness.

The threshold of adolescence is marked by the recognition that one or another of the elements of one's previous child-identity no longer fits, and the effect of adolescence is, so to speak, to place a question mark beside each of the aspects of the identity one bore as a child. To be reared a Presbyterian, for example, is for the child to be a Presbyterian; but for the adolescent, to have been reared a Presbyterian is to pose the question of one's present and future relationship to Presbyterianism.

The threshold of adolescence is marked also by a strong inner urge, namely, the urge to overleap the fences that marked off one's prior childhood as a protected clearing. This urge is developmentally sound, because with respect to the familiar situations of one's childhood, one has been conditioned in what to think and feel. On fresh ground, adolescents experience novel ideas and feelings, amid which they can expect to find some that are their own in a sense that the thoughts and feelings of their childhood are now recognizably no longer their own. By finding these and identifying with them, adolescents begin to live their own life, in preparation for making their own life-shaping choices.

The shared thesis of the philosophies of life I have referred to is that persons who experience intrinsic rewards at what they do invest the best of themselves in it and realize objective values—values that can be appreciated and utilized by other persons. These intrinsic rewards were termed *eudaimonia* by the ancient Greeks, which can be translated as the distinctive kind of happiness associated with self-fulfilling living. Accordingly, I mean by worthy living—living that realizes objective value and at the same time is self-fulfilling to the individual whose life it is. As the Greeks recognized, to generalize the opportunity for such living requires supportive social institutions, and I will now condense what I have been saying about the education of our young into two criteria and add just a few words about implementation.

At the level of elementary education, the paramount consideration must be to keep the intrinsic rewards of learning alive. This is partly because the self-discovery in adolescence that initiates the development of self-knowledge depends upon the ability in persons to distinguish intrinsically rewarding courses of conduct from those that do not afford intrinsic rewards. It is also because the continuous growth that characterizes a well-lived adulthood, and includes continuous learning, must be fueled by intrinsic rewards.

It has been said that the code of every caring profession must begin with *Primum non nocere*, "First of all, do no harm." By my argument, in education this means, "Don't destroy the intrinsic rewards of learning and growth that are evident in every infant and small child." In Abraham Maslow's botanical image, "Don't step on the growth tip."[14]

At the secondary and college level, what is required is to facilitate exploration for the purpose of self-discovery followed by steadily growing self-knowledge. When a person's life-shaping choices are based in solid self-knowledge, the likelihood is markedly increased that in later life the individual will perceive the rightness of the course of life he or she is living. By contrast, the prevalence among us of what is termed "midlife crises" reflects, I think, some measure of regret in persons regarding some of their life-shaping choices. The prevalence is unsurprising given the neglect of the matter of self-knowledge by our pattern of education and by our society generally.

What is required to support the acquisition of self-knowledge by our students at the secondary and college levels is opportunity for exploration, and this requires a variety of situations. Young people should be looking for situations, courses of conduct, and relationships that they experience as intrinsically rewarding, because this identifies their potentialities. Variety of situations cannot be provided in classrooms, because the classroom is itself an imposing situation whose existential tonality, or "flavor," masks the existential tonalities of whatever is brought into it.

Accordingly, the aim of self-knowledge entails breaking up our pattern of education as sixteen-years-at-one-sitting. In the words of former secretary of labor Willard Wirtz, it requires breaking up the "time traps of youth for education, adulthood for work, old age for nothing."[15] An excellent start is President Clinton's proposal for a National Service program—an idea that was originally proposed eighty years ago by William James in his essay "The Moral Equivalent of War,"[16] and that has since received vigorous support from, among others, Margaret Mead, Theodore Hesburgh, Erik Erikson, Presidents Roosevelt, Kennedy, and Johnson, and two years ago from Senators Sam Nunn and Barbara Mikulski.[17] A National Service program should include international exchanges of work parties and should be complemented by generalized use of apprenticeships and internships, and of work-study programs in which semesters in the classroom are alternated with semesters of exploratory work in the larger society. The effect would be to address the wise finding of the Carnegie Council study on education, *Giving Youth a Better Chance*. The study found that "young people receive too heavy a dose of schooling for too long a period, unmixed with knowledge of the world of work or experience in work or community service. Work that takes the form of community service is particularly desirable, giving young people a feeling of involvement in community problems and of contributing to their solution."[18]

To be sure, the idea of a year or two of national service, say between high school and college, arouses the anxiety that many young people will not return to their formal education or will lose their study skills. But it is a matter of wide agreement that the best wave of students to pass through our colleges and universities was that of the returning G. I.s from World War II—men and women whose military service separated them from formal studies for from two to four years. Their academic rustiness was but a trifling challenge to their enhanced maturity and heightened resolve.

But as Socrates said, a person must have an idea of what he or she is looking for in order to recognize it when he or she finds it. What young people should be looking for are situations, courses of conduct, and relationships that they experience as intrinsically rewarding. To do this they must know what intrinsic rewards are, and this means that the intrinsic rewards of learning and growth must have been prominent in their elementary and secondary education.

The way to preserve the intrinsic rewards of learning and growth in elementary and secondary education is by including the spontaneous interests of children and young people in the curriculum. The effect of this is to make their classrooms their place, not an alien environment geared to turning out "classroom products," against which the more spirited students, as Theodore Sizer noted, protect themselves by dis-identifying with their classrooms and identifying themselves instead with some other dimension of their lives.

Let us suppose that part of the class day in our hypothetical elementary school classroom is devoted to the spontaneous interests of individual children—two or three today, one or two others tomorrow, two or three others the next day, and so on. What happens to the rest of the school day? The rest of it is devoted familiarly to what adults perceive that children need to learn. But it is the responsibility of every teacher to first use his or her ingenuity to provoke in children the curiosity to learn what the prescribed studies are meant to teach. It is this ability, before all others, that should define "teaching excellence." Never should a new subject be introduced with those deadening words "You will need to know this." In the sound pedagogical advice of Kurt Hahn, founder both of Gordonstoun School in Scotland and of Outward Bound, to fail to elicit first the interest is to present "a hook without a worm."

To arouse first interest is challenging but not daunting, for the minds of children are fluid and impulsive and can be set off at a gallop with a little inducement. One school I know uses a steady stream of guests from the community for this purpose. I was there one day when the visitor was a mountaineer who showed breathtaking photographs of the first American ascent of the mountain K-2 on the China-Afghanistan border, in which he participated. At the time he spoke, cartographers were making the first accurate measurements of the height of K-2, and it was thought that it might prove to be taller than Mount Everest. Many children became interested in how the height of mountains is measured, and because triangulation is involved, they were led to the study of trigonometry. A week later interest in psychology was aroused by a police captain's reflections on the question of "the criminal mind."

A technique for engaging interest in what is to be learned is to work with children to construct an imaginary situation in which children, by what I will term *participatory enactment*, arrive at their need to know. Every caring parent and teacher makes occasional use of this method, but it has been developed to a remarkable degree by the Jordanhill College of Education in Glasgow, Scotland, whose computer-assisted "topic studies" are now in use in every public elementary school in Scotland.[19] The topic study "Desperate Journey," for example, begins at the croft of a Highland family in the last century. The children model the setting, the family members, and the livestock and imaginatively develop the scene in great detail while learning basic principles of agriculture, arithmetic, accounting, and much else. Then the family is evicted by the Highland Clearances, and the children study the history of this event from several points of view. But where will the family go? It moves to

Glasgow, but mother is ill and father does not find work. How will they survive? The children must take work in a weaving mill, and everything from weaving and the industrial revolution to detailed historical records of Glasgow in the period are studied in the order that is determined by the children's felt need to know. But the family endures this situation only until it can manage to migrate to Canada. Now ship construction is studied, models are made and floated, and what is meant by "pitch," "roll," and "yaw" are learned by sending waves against the models. Elementary principles of navigation are studied, relations with captain and crew are examined, and much else. I will not follow the family to its new home in Canada, but conclude by noting that a study can last an entire semester, that what can be taught by this means puts to shame the rote learning "Because you will need to know this" of too many traditional classrooms, and that students who have been questioned a year after the conclusion of a given topic study demonstrate complete—and enthusiastic—recall.[20]

On the basis of my observations in elementary and secondary classrooms in America and abroad over the past five years, my conclusion is that preserving the intrinsic rewards of learning and growing is a matter not of discovering how this can be done but of recognizing the importance of doing so. My argument has been that the quality of living, from childhood through old age, is at stake.

Notes

1. National Commission of Excellence in Education, *A Nation at Risk: The Imperative for Educational Reform* (Washington, D.C.: U.S. Government Printing Office, 1983), p. 5.

2. A collation of these findings is Robert S. Siegler, *Children's Thinking* (Englewood Cliffs, N.J.: Prentice-Hall, 1986).

3. Theodore R. Sizer, *Horace's Compromise: The Dilemma of the American High School* (Boston: Houghton Mifflin, 1984), pp. 54–55.

4. Alfred North Whitehead, *The Aims of Education and Other Essays* (New York: The Free Press, 1967), p. 16.

5. Michael Bend, "A Brief Description of the Newark Center for Creative Learning," in *Compulsory Schooling and Human Learning: The*

Moral Failure of Public Education in America and Japan, ed. Dayle M. Bethel (San Francisco: Caddo Gap Press, in press).

6. Kuniko Kato, "Children's Village: The Evolution of an Alternative School," in *Compulsory Schooling and Human Learning: The Moral Failure of Public Education in America and Japan*, ed. Dayle M. Bethel (San Francisco: Caddo Gap Press, in press).

7. This is a good place to indicate my recognition that our public schools include many wise, dedicated, and resourceful teachers. Most that I have spoken with, however, express keen frustration at persistent thwarting of their best endeavors by school administrators, or just "the system."

8. This problem is documented in many studies summarized by Linda M. McNeil, "Contradictions of Control, Part 1: Administrators and Teachers," *Phi Delta Kappan* 69, no. 5 (January 1988): 333–39. The studies show that teacher input, always minute, diminished to the vanishing point after Sputnik triggered the "space war" between America and the USSR. Among extended studies stressing this point is Douglas A. Archibald and Andrew Porter, "Curriculum Control and Teachers' Perception of Autonomy and Satisfaction," *Educational Evaluation and Policy Analysis* 16, no. 1: 21–40.

9. For this history, see Harry Braverman, *Labor and Monopoly Capital: The Degradation of Work in the Twentieth Century* (New York: Monthly Review Press, 1974). For the extrapolation of this trend to the thesis that it is management's responsibility to shape the character and values of workers, see William G. Scott, *Chester I. Barnard and the Guardians of the Managerial State* (Lawrence, Kans.: University Press of Kansas, 1992).

10. *Encyclopedia Britannica*, 15th ed., s.v. "Taylor, Frederick W."

11. See Raymond E. Callahan, *Education and the Cult of Efficiency: A Study of the Social Forces That Have Shaped the Administration of the Public Schools* (Chicago: University of Chicago Press, 1962).

12. Robert Louis Stevenson, "Letter to a Young Gentleman," in *Across the Plains, with Other Memories and Essays* (New York: Scribner's Sons, 1904), p. 272.

13. James C. Coleman, "The School to Work Transition," in *The Teenage Employment Problem: What Are the Options?* issued by the U.S. Congressional Budget Office (Washington, D.C.: U.S. Government Printing Office, 1976), pp. 35–40.

14. Abraham Maslow, in conversation.

15. Willard Wirtz and National Manpower Institute, *The Boundless Resource: A Prospectus for an Education-Work Policy* (Washington, D.C.: New Republic Books, 1975), p. 9.

16. William James, "The Moral Equivalent of War, in *Essays in Religion and Morality* (Cambridge, Mass.: Harvard University Press, 1982), pp. 162–73.

17. A history of the National Service idea is Michael W. Sherraden and Donald Eberly, *National Service: Social, Economic, and Military Impacts* (New York: Pergamon Press, 1981).

18. Carnegie Council Report, *Giving Youth a Better Chance* (San Francisco: Jossey-Bass, 1979), 94–95.

19. Literature is available from the director of sales and publications at Jordanhill College of Education, 76 Southbrae Drive, Glasgow G13 1PP, Scotland.

20. As reported by my wife, Mary K. Norton, from her observations of a dozen Scottish elementary schools in 1990.

REFERENCES

INDEX

References

Abbey, Edward. *Desert Solitaire*. New York: Ballantine Books, 1968.

Amory, Cleveland. *Man Kind? Our Incredible War on Wildlife*. New York: Harper & Row, 1974.

Archibald, Douglas A., and Andrew Porter. "Curriculum Control and Teachers' Perception of Autonomy and Satisfaction." *Educational Evaluation and Policy Analysis* 16, no. 1: 21–40.

Austin, Philip. *Our Duty Towards Animals*. London: Kegan Paul, Trench & Co., 1885.

Baier, Kurt. *The Moral Point of View*. New York: Random House, 1965.

Bend, Michael. "A Brief Description of the Newark Center for Creative Learning." In *Compulsory Schooling and Human Learning: The Moral Failure of Public Education in America and Japan*, ed. Dayle M. Bethel. San Francisco: Caddo Gap Press, in press.

Benjamin, Martin. "Ethics and Animal Consciousness." In *Social Ethics*, eds. Thomas Mappes and Jane Zembaty, pp. 394–401. Englewood Cliffs, N.J.: Prentice-Hall, 1982.

Benn, Stanley I., and Richard Stanley Peters. *The Principles of Political Thought*. New York: The Free Press, 1965.

Bentham, Jeremy. *Introduction to the Principles of Morals and Legislation*. London: T. Payne, 1789. Reprint, ed. J. H. Burns and H. L. A. Hart, London: Athlone Press, University of London, 1970.

Berlin, Isaiah. *Four Essays on Liberty*. London and New York: Oxford University Press, 1969.

————. "Two Concepts of Liberty." In *Four Essays on Liberty*, pp. 118–72. Oxford: Oxford University Press, 1970.

Birke, Lynda. *Women, Feminism, and Biology: The Feminist Challenge*. London: Routledge, Chapman & Hall, 1986.

Braverman, Harry. *Labor and Monopoly Capital: The Degradation of Work in the Twentieth Century*. New York: Monthly Review Press, 1974.

Callahan, Raymond E. *Education and the Cult of Efficiency: A Study of the Social Forces That Have Shaped the Administration of the Public Schools*. Chicago: University of Chicago Press, 1962.

Carnegie Council Report. *Giving Youth a Better Chance*. San Francisco: Jossey-Bass, 1979.

Coleman, James C. "The School to Work Transition." In *The Teenage Employment Problem: What Are the Options?* issued by the U.S. Congressional Budget Office, pp. 35–40. Washington, D.C.: U.S. Government Printing Office, 1976.

Cranston, Maurice. *Freedom: A New Analysis*. New York: Longmans, Green, 1953.

Crocker, Lawrence. *Positive Liberty*. The Hague: Matinus Nijhoff, 1980.

Cyon, Elie De. "The Anti-Vivisectionist Agitation." *Contemporary Review* 43 (1883): 498–510.

Dawkins, Richard. *The Selfish Gene*. Oxford: Oxford University Press, 1976.

Descartes, René. *Discourse on Method*. In *The Philosophical Works of Descartes*, 2 vols., trans. Elizabeth Haldane and G. R. T. Ross, vol. 1, pp. 79–130. Cambridge: Cambridge University Press, 1991.

Douglas, Mary. *Purity and Danger: An Analysis of Concepts of Pollution and Taboo*. London: Routledge & Kegan Paul, 1966.

Feinberg, Joel. *Rights, Justice, and the Bounds of Liberty*. Princeton: Princeton University Press, 1980.

————. *Social Philosophy*. Englewood Cliffs, N.J.: Prentice-Hall, 1973.

————, ed. *Reason and Responsibility*, 6th ed. Belmont, Calif.: Wadsworth Publishing Co., 1985.

Fontaine, Nicholas. *The Fables of La Fontaine*. Trans. Marianne Moore. New York: Viking Press, 1952.

Frankena, William. "Obligation and Ability." In *Philosophical*

Analysis, ed. Max Black, pp. 157–75. Ithaca, N.Y.: Cornell University Press, 1950.

French, Marilyn. *Beyond Power: Of Women, Men, and Morals.* New York: Ballantine Books, 1986.

Freuchen, Peter. *Book of the Eskimos.* New York: World Publishing Co., 1961.

Frey, R. G. *Interests and Rights: The Case Against Animal Rights.* Oxford: Clarendon Press, 1980.

———. *Rights, Killing, and Suffering.* Oxford: Basil Blackwell, 1983.

Gearhart, Sally M. "An End to Technology: A Modest Proposal." In *Machina Ex Dea: Feminist Perspectives on Technology*, ed. Joan Rothschild, pp. 171–83. New York: Pergamon Press, 1983.

Gilligan, Carol. *In a Different Voice: Psychological Theory and Women's Development.* Cambridge, Mass.: Harvard University Press, 1982.

Gillis, John S. *Too Tall, Too Small.* Champaign, Ill.: Institute for Personality and Ability Testing, 1982.

Goldman, Alvin. *A Theory of Human Action.* Englewood Cliffs, N.J.: Prentice-Hall, 1970.

Gould, Carol C. *Rethinking Democracy: Freedom and Social Cooperation in Politics, Economy, and Society.* New York: Cambridge University Press, 1988.

Haldane, Elizabeth S., and G. R. T. Ross, trans. *The Philosophical Works of Descartes.* 2 vols. New York: Dover Books, 1955.

Held, Virginia. *Rights and Goods.* New York: The Free Press, 1984.

Helvétius, Claude Adrien. *A Treatise on Man.* 2 vols. Paris: Chez la Société Typographique, 1773.

Hobbes, Thomas. *Leviathan.* New York: Collier Books, 1962.

Hospers, John. *Libertarianism.* Los Angeles: Nash Publishers, 1971.

James, William. "The Moral Equivalent of War." In *Essays in Religion and Morality*, pp. 162–73. Cambridge, Mass.: Harvard University Press, 1982.

Kahane, Howard. "Making the World Safe for Reciprocity." In *Reason and Responsibility*, ed. Joel Feinberg, 6th ed., pp. 495–502. Belmont, Calif.: Wadsworth Publishing Co., 1985.

Kant, Immanuel. *Lectures on Ethics*, trans. Louis Infield. New York: Harper & Row, 1963.

Kato, Kuniko. "Children's Village: The Evolution of an Alternative School." In *Compulsory Schooling and Human Learning: The Moral Failure of Public Education in America and Japan*, ed. Dayle M. Bethel. San Francisco: Caddo Gap Press, in press.

Kleinig, John. *Valuing Life*. Princeton, N.J.: Princeton University Press, 1991.

La Fontaine, Jean. *The Fables of La Fontaine*. Trans. Marianne Moore. New York: Viking Press, 1952.

Leopold, Aldo. *Sand County Almanac*. Oxford: Oxford University Press, 1949.

Lombardi, Louis. "Inherent Worth, Respect, and Rights." *Environmental Ethics* 5 (fall 1983): 257–70.

Lovelock, James, and Sidney Epton. "The Quest of Gaia." *New Scientist* 65 (February 6, 1975): 304–9.

MacCallum, Gerald. "Negative and Positive Freedom." *Philosophical Review* 76, no. 3 (July 1967): 312–34.

Machan, Tibor R. *Human Rights and Human Liberties*. Chicago: Nelson Hall, 1975.

Mackie, J. L. "The Law of the Jungle: Moral Alternatives and Principles of Evolution." *Philosophy* 53 (October 1978): 455–64.

Macpherson, Crawford Brough. *Democratic Theory: Essays in Retrieval*. Oxford: Oxford University Press, 1973.

Mappes, Thomas, and Jane Zembaty, eds. *Social Ethics*. 2d ed. Englewood Cliffs, N.J.: Prentice-Hall, 1982.

McComas, Maggie, and others. *The Dilemma of Third World Nutrition*. N.p.: Nestle, 1983.

McNeil, Linda M. "Contradictions of Control, Part 1: Administrators and Teachers." *Phi Delta Kappan* 69, no. 5 (January 1988): 333–39.

McPhee, Carol, and Ann FitsGerald, eds. *Feminist Quotations: Voices of Rebels, Reformers, and Visionaries*. New York: Crowell, 1979.

Moore, George Edward. *Principia Ethica*. Cambridge, Mass.: Cambridge University Press, 1903.

National Commission of Excellence in Education. *A Nation at Risk: The Imperative for Educational Reform*. Washington, D.C.: U.S. Government Printing Office, 1983.

Nielson, Kai. "Why Should I Be Moral? Revisited." *American Philosophical Quarterly* 1, no. 21 (January 1984): 81–91.

Phillips, M. T., and J. Sechzer. *Animal Research and Ethical Conflict*. New York: Springer-Verlag, 1989.

Plumwood, Val. "Women, Humanity, and Nature." *Radical Philosophy* 48 (1988): 16–24.

Pojman, Louis P. "A Critique of Contemporary Egalitarianism." *Faith and Philosophy* 8, no. 4 (October 1991): 481–504.

———. *Ethics: Discovering Right and Wrong*. Belmont, Calif.: Wadsworth Publishing Co., 1990.

———. *Life and Death: Grappling with the Moral Dilemmas of Our Time*. Boston: Jones & Bartlett, 1992.

———. "The Moral Status of Affirmative Action." *Public Affairs Quarterly* 6, no. 2 (April 1992): 181–206.

Rasmussen, Knud. *The People of the Polar North*. London: Kegan Paul, Trench, Trubner & Co., 1908.

Regan, Tom. *The Case for Animal Rights*. Berkeley, Calif.: University of California Press, 1983.

———. "The Case for Animal Rights." In *In Defense of Animals*, ed. Peter Singer, pp. 13–26. Oxford: Basil Blackwell, 1985.

———, ed. *Matters of Life and Death*. New York: Random House, 1980.

Reusch, Hans. *Top of the World*. New York: Pocket Books, 1951.

Rothschild, Joan, ed. *Machina Ex Dea: Feminist Perspectives on Technology*. New York: Pergamon Press, 1983.

Salleh, Ariel Kay. "Contributing to the Critique of Political Epistemology." *Thesis Eleven* 8 (1984): 23–43.

Scanlon, T. M. "Contractualism and Utilitarianism." In *Utilitarianism and Beyond*, ed. Sen Amartya and others, pp. 103–28. London: Cambridge University Press, 1982.

Scott, William G. *Chester I. Barnard and the Guardians of the Managerial State*. Lawrence, Kans.: University Press of Kansas, 1992.

Sherraden, Michael W., and Donald Eberly. *National Service: Social, Economic, and Military Impacts*. New York: Pergamon Press, 1981.

Siegler, Robert S. *Children's Thinking*. Englewood Cliffs, N.J.: Prentice-Hall, 1986.

Singer, Peter. "Animal Liberation." *New York Review of Books* April 5, 1973, pp. 17–21.

———. *Animal Liberation*. New York: Avon, 1976.

————. "Animals and the Value of Life." In *Matters of Life and Death*, ed. Tom Regan, pp. 218–59. New York: Random House, 1980.

————. *Practical Ethics*. Cambridge: Cambridge University Press, 1980.

Singer, Peter, and Tom Regan, eds. *Animal Rights and Human Obligations*. Englewood Cliffs, N.J.: Prentice-Hall, 1976.

Sizer, Theodore R. *Horace's Compromise: The Dilemma of the American High School*. Boston: Houghton Mifflin, 1984.

Sterba, James P. *How to Make People Just: A Practical Reconciliation of Alternative Conceptions of Justice*. Totowa, N.J.: Roman & Littlefield, 1988.

————. "Is There a Rationale for Punishment?" *American Journal of Jurisprudence* 29 (1984): 29–43.

————. "Moral Approaches to Nuclear Strategy: A Critical Evaluation." *Canadian Journal of Philosophy* 12, supp. 12 (1986): 75–109.

————. "Neo-Libertarianism." *American Philosophical Quarterly* 15 (April 1978): 115–21.

————. "The Welfare Rights of Distant Peoples and Future Generations: Moral Side-Constraints on Social Policy." *Social Theory and Practice* 7 (spring 1981): 99–119.

Stevenson, Robert Louis. "Letter to a Young Gentleman." In *Across the Plains, with Other Memories and Essays*, pp. 272–88. New York: Scribner's Sons, 1904.

Stitch, Stephen. "Do Animals Have Beliefs?" *Australasian Journal of Philosophy* 57, no. 1 (March 1979): 15–28.

Taylor, Paul. "The Ethics of Respect for Nature." *Environmental Ethics* 3 (fall 1981): 197–218.

————. *Respect for Nature*. Princeton, N.J.: Princeton University Press, 1986.

Thomas Aquinas. *Summa Contra Gentiles*. London: Benziger Brothers, 1928.

————. *Summa Theologica*. London: Benziger Brothers, 1918.

Tolstoy, Leo. "Religion and Morality." In *Leo Tolstoy, Selected Essays*, pp. 7–32. New York: Modern Library, 1964.

Trotsky, Leon. *Literature and Revolution*, trans. Rose Strunsky. Ann Arbor, Mich.: University of Michigan Press, 1960.

U.S. Congress. Office of Technology. *Alternatives to Animal Use in Research, Testing, and Education*. New York: Dekker, 1988.

U.S. House Subcommittee of International Economic Policy

and Trade of the Committee on Foreign Affairs. *Marketing and Promotion of Infant Formula in Developing Countries: Hearing Before the Subcommittee of International Economic Policy and Trade of the Committee on Foreign Affairs.* 96th Cong., 2d sess., 1980.

VanDeVeer, Donald, and Christine Pierce, eds. "Interspecific Justice." In *People, Penguins, and Plastic Trees*, pp. 51–66. Belmont, Calif.: Wadsworth Publishing Co., 1986.

———. *People, Penguins, and Plastic Trees.* Belmont, Calif.: Wadsworth Publishing Co., 1986.

Warren, Mary Anne. "Difficulties with the Strong Animal Rights Position." *Between the Species* 2, no. 4 (fall 1987): 163–73.

Whitehead, Alfred North. *The Aims of Education and Other Essays.* New York: The Free Press, 1967.

Wirtz, Willard, and National Manpower Institute. *The Boundless Resource: A Prospectus for an Education-Work Policy.* Washington, D.C.: New Republic Books, 1975.

Wollstonecraft, Mary. *A Vindication of the Rights of Women.* London: Dent, 1982.

Index

185

JOHN HOWIE, professor of philosophy at Southern Illinois University at Carbondale, received his Ph.D. degree from Boston University. He is the author of *Perspectives for Moral Decisions*, the editor of *Ethical Principles for Social Policy* and *Ethical Principles and Practice*, and the coeditor of *Contemporary Studies in Philosophical Idealism* and *The Wisdom of William Ernest Hocking*. He has published articles in *The Philosophical Forum*, *Stylus*, *Contemporary Philosophy*, *The Personalist Forum*, *Idealistic Studies*, *Religious Studies*, *Dialectics and Humanism*, *The Journal of Social Philosophy*, and *Indian Philosophical Quarterly*.

GEORGE SCHEDLER, professor of philosophy at Southern Illinois University at Carbondale, received his Ph.D. from the University of California, San Diego, and his J.D. (*cum laude*) from Southern Illinois University School of Law. He is the author of *Introductory Symbolic Logic* and *Behavior Modification and Punishment of the Innocent*. Among the articles he has written are "Capital Punishment and Its Deterrent Effects," first published in *Social Theory and Practice* and later reprinted in Richard Wasserstrom's *Today's Moral Problems* and in Ralph Clark's *Introduction to Moral Reasoning*, and "Hobbes on the Basis of Political Obligation," first published in *Journal of the History of Philosophy* and later reprinted in Preston King's *Thomas Hobbes: Critical Assessments*.